the epic world's best JOKES for kids

LISA SWERLING & RALPH LAZAR

A special collection featuring jokes from
The World's Best Jokes for Kids Volume 1,
The World's Best Jokes for Kids Volume 2, and
The World's Best Dad Jokes for Kids Volume 3

Andrews McMeel
PUBLISHING®

Andrews McMeel Publishing
a division of Andrews McMeel Universal
1130 Walnut Street, Kansas City, Missouri 64106

www.andrewsmcmeel.com

24 25 26 27 28 LAK 10 9 8 7 6 5 4 3 2 1

ISBN: 979-8-8816-0000-6

Editor: Cindy Harris
Art Director: Abby Gust Hutter
Production Editor: Brianna Westervelt
Production Manager: Shona Burns

ATTENTION: SCHOOLS AND BUSINESSES
Andrews McMeel books are available at quantity discounts with bulk purchase for educational, business, or sales promotional use. For information, please e-mail the Andrews McMeel Publishing Special Sales Department:
sales@amuniversal.com.

This book is for

Gabriel + Jamie

Siena + Dash

and all the other
joke-tellers out there,
young and old.

What is heavy and wears glass slippers?

Cinderelephant.

What did the principal say to the misbehaving egg?

You're egg-spelled!

Which is the most magical dog?

A labracadabrador.

What do you call a bear with no ears?

B.

You can tune a guitar.

But you can't tuna fish.

What do you call a
bee that comes from
America?

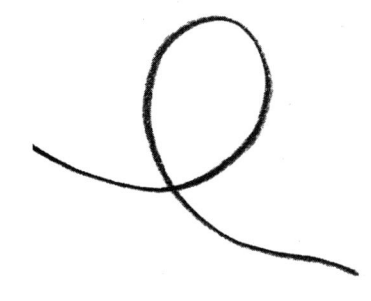

 USB.

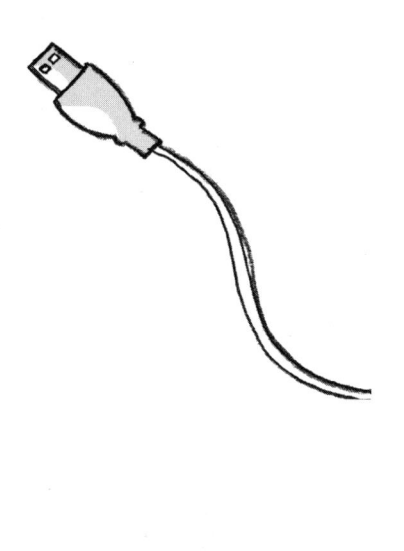

Why can't you give
Elsa a balloon?

Because she'll
let it go.

What do you call an elephant that doesn't matter?

An irrelephant.

What did the buffalo say when he dropped his son off at school?

Bison.

What do you call an ant that won't go away?

Permanant.

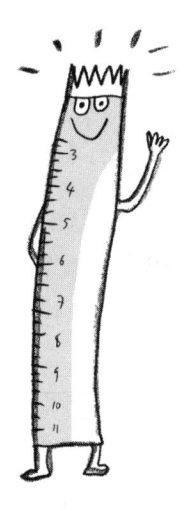

Why was the king only 12 inches tall?

Because he was a ruler.

How do you describe a person with no body and just a nose?

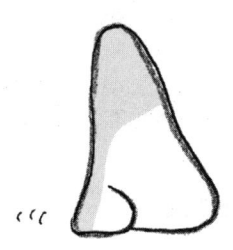

Nobody nose.

I was wondering, why does a frisbee appear larger the closer it gets?

Then it hit me.

What do you call the new girl at the bank?

The nutella.

Did you hear about the hungry clock?

It went back four seconds.

Why do seagulls fly over the sea and not the bay?

Because otherwise they'd be bagels.

Why are pirates called pirates?

Because they arrrrrrr.

What do you call having your granny on speed dial?

Instagran.

What happened to the dog that swallowed a firefly?

It barked with de-light!

What treat is never on time?

Choco-late.

What do you call a bear with no teeth?

A gummy bear.

What is E.T. short for?

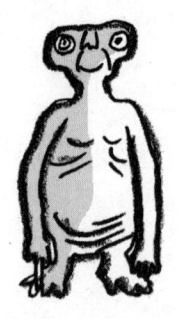

Because he's got such little legs.

Why did the robber take a bath?

He wanted to make a clean getaway.

How do you make an octopus laugh?

With ten-tickles.

What do you call a nervous
javelin thrower?

Shakespeare.

Where do crayons
go on vacation?

Color-ado.

What do you
call a belt with
a clock on it?

A waist of time.

Why did the giraffe
get bad grades?

She always had her head
in the clouds.

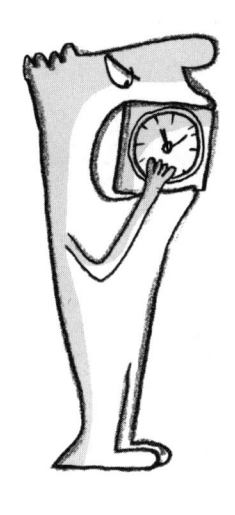

Have you ever
tried to eat
a clock?

It's very time
consuming.

What did the blanket
say to the bed?

"Don't worry,
I've got you
covered."

What did the one snail
say to the other?

"It's about
slime we started dating."

What do you call a positive bunny?

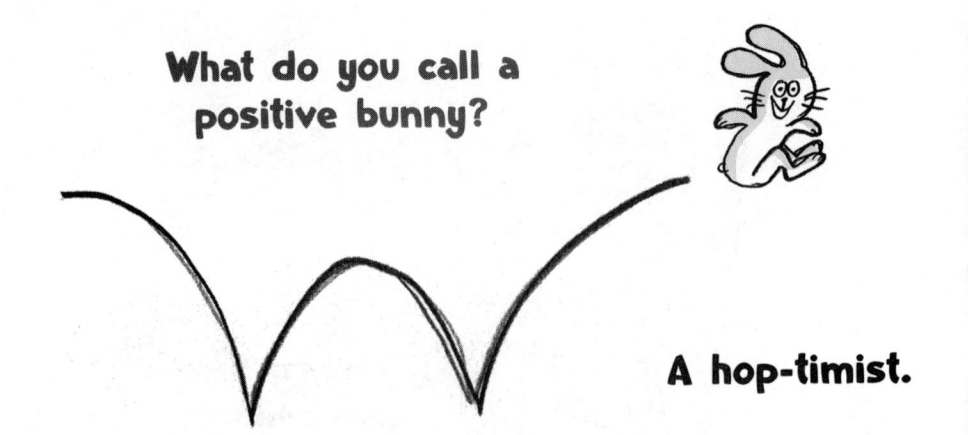

A hop-timist.

What kind of math do birds like?

Owlgebra.

What do sea monsters eat?

Fish & ships.

Why did the horse keep
falling over?

He just wasn't stable.

Why did the
traffic light
turn red?

You would too if you had to change
on the side of the road.

I've just returned from a once-in-a-lifetime vacation.

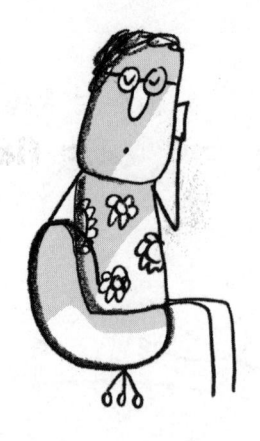

Never again.

Why was six scared of seven?

Because seven ate nine.

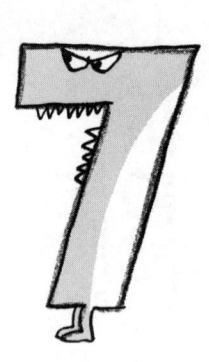

I hate Russian dolls.

So full of themselves.

What's the best thing about Switzerland?

I don't know, but their flag is a huge plus.

What did the one fish say to the other?

"Hey, long time no sea."

Why did the tomato blush?

It saw the salad dressing.

What do you give a horse with a cold?

Cough stirrup.

What did Bacon say to Tomato?

"Lettuce get together!"

**Why don't skeletons
fight each other?**

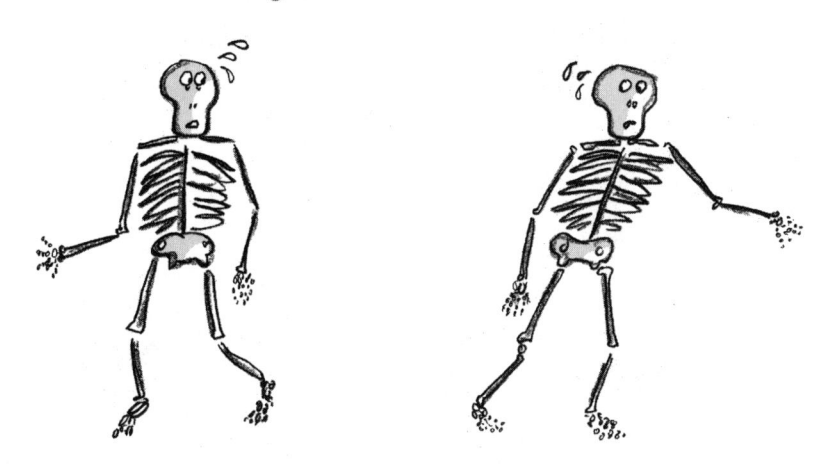

They just don't have the guts.

**What do you call a line of
men waiting for a haircut?**

A barbeque.

What did the dad chimney say to the little chimney?

"You're too young to smoke!"

What dog keeps the best time?

A watch dog.

What do you get when you cross a monkey with a peach?

An ape-ricot.

What happens when you annoy a rabbit?

You have a bad hare day.

What kind of lights did Noah use on the ark?

Flood lights.

Time flies like an arrow.

Fruit flies like a banana.

What's the best kind of snack to eat during a horror movie?

I scream.

Why was the bed wearing a disguise?

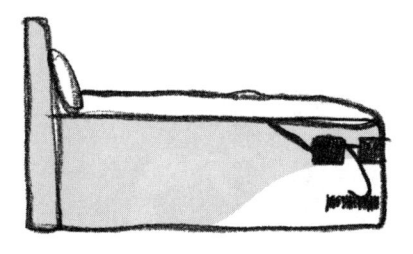

Because it was under cover.

 Did you hear about the smelly fairy?

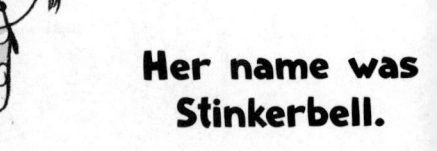 Her name was Stinkerbell.

Who brings kittens for Christmas?

Santa claws.

The teacher shouted at me for something I didn't do.

What was it?

My homework.

What did the martian say
to the flower bed?

"Take me to your
weeder!"

Did you hear about the actress
who fell through the floor?

It was just a stage she
was going through.

When do you
stop on green
and go on red?

When you're
eating watermelon.

Who helped the monster
go to the ball?

Its scary
godmother.

Did you hear about
the restaurant on Mars?

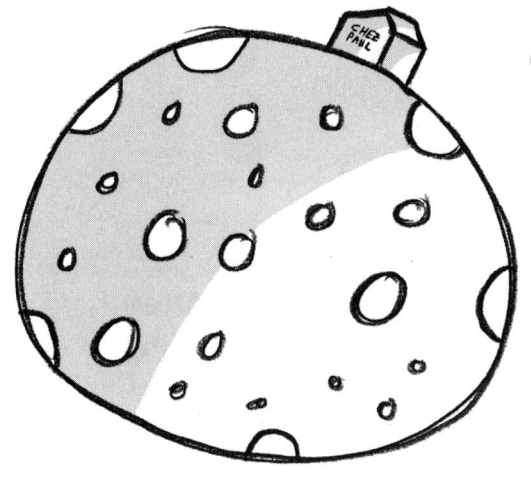

Great food but no
atmosphere.

Why did the girl's parents scream
when they saw her grades?

Because she had a bee
on her report card.

Why do flamingos stand on one leg?

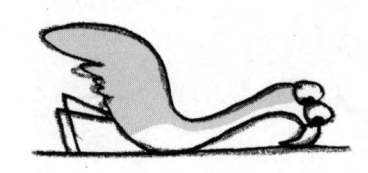

Because if they lifted it, they'd fall over.

How did the french fry propose to the hamburger?

He gave her an onion ring.

How do you stop a dog from barking in
the back seat of the car?

Put him in the front seat
of the car.

What do peanut
butter and jelly
do around the
campfire?

They tell toast stories.

What do you get when you cross
a pig with a millipede?

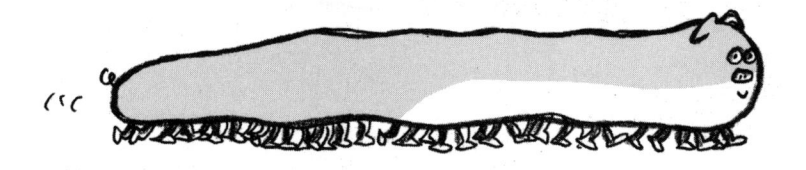

Bacon and legs.

What do you call a bear standing in the rain?

A drizzly bear.

What did the mother corn say to her kids?

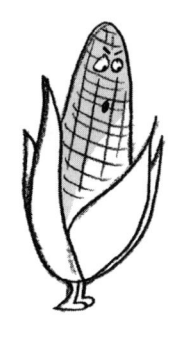

"Don't forget to clean behind your ears."

What is the craziest way to travel?

By loco-motive.

Why did the ninja spend the day in bed?

He had kung-flu.

Why did the cookie complain about being sick?

He was feeling crummy.

What is a baby's motto?

If at first you don't succeed, cry, cry again.

"You missed school yesterday."

"To tell you the truth, I didn't really miss it."

What happens if you eat yeast and shoe polish?

You'll rise and shine every morning!

What do you call an alligator in a vest?

An investigator.

What do you call a fake noodle?

An Impasta.

Where do rabbits go after their wedding?

On a bunny-moon.

**Why did the little birdie
fly to the hospital?**

To get tweetment.

**What is extremely heavy,
has 6 wheels, and flies?**

A garbage truck.

**How did the
snail get a view
of New York City?**

By shell-icopter.

**Why did the man jump up and
down before drinking his juice?**

**The instructions on the carton said,
"Shake well before drinking."**

What do you call spiders on honeymoon?

Newlywebs.

What did the tree say to the flower?

"I'm rooting for you."

**Why did the
man run around
his bed?**

**Because he was trying to
catch up on his sleep.**

**Can a flea
jump higher
than a bus?**

Of course! Buses can't jump.

Why wouldn't the monster eat the clown?

Because he suspected it would taste funny.

Why are ghosts such bad liars?

Because you can see right through them.

Why did the math book look so sad?

It had lots of problems.

What did one wall say to the other?

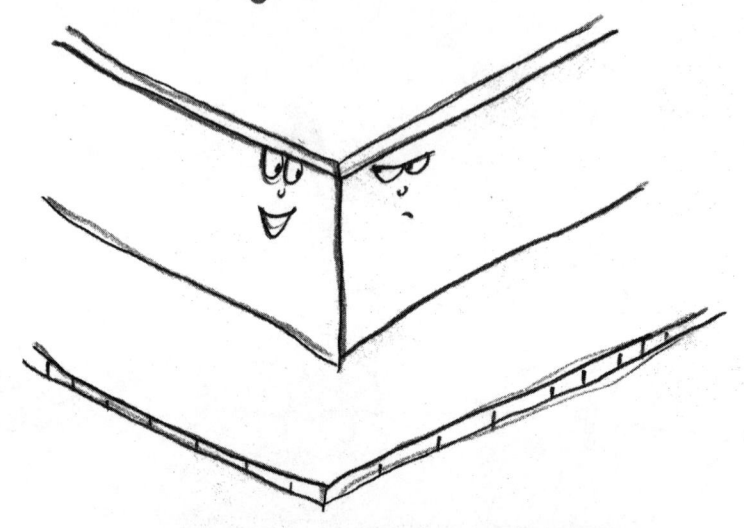

"Let's meet at the corner."

What does a rain cloud wear under its clothes?

Thunderwear.

Why did the banana wear sunscreen on the beach?

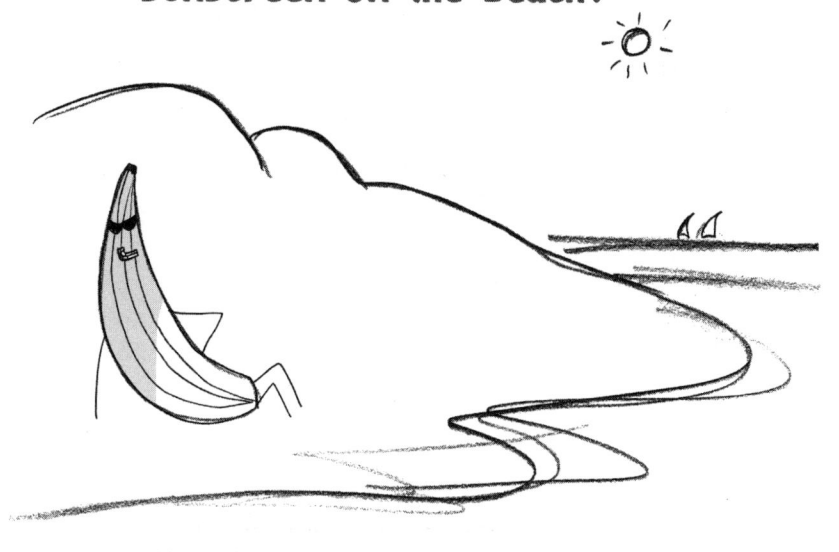

He didn't want to peel.

**How did the
baseball player
lose his house?**

**He made his
home run.**

**Why did the golfer wear
two pairs of pants?**

In case he got a hole in one.

Why was everyone looking up and cheering?

They were ceiling fans.

Slept like a log last night.

Woke up in the fireplace.

What do you call a pig that knows karate?

A pork chop.

Did you hear about the claustrophobic astronaut?

He just needed space.

Why was the broom late for school?

Because it over swept.

Why was the nose feeling sad?

Because it was tired of being picked on.

What nursery rhyme do camels like best?

Humpty Dumpty.

What do you call a dentist who fixes crocodiles' teeth?

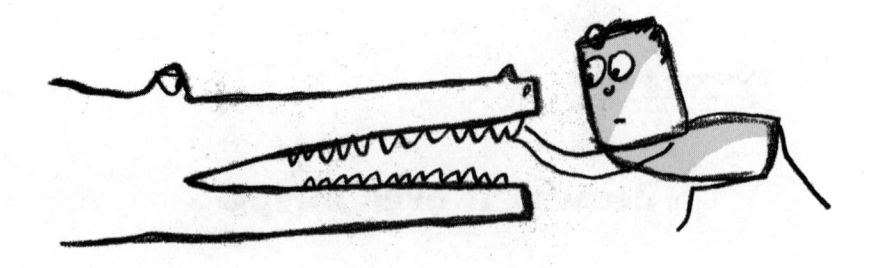

Totally crazy.

Did you hear about the teacher who was cross-eyed?

He couldn't control his pupils.

Why couldn't the monster get to sleep?

Because it was afraid that there were children under the bed.

What stays in the corner yet travels across the world?

Ben + Eileen Dover
13 Avocado Avenue
Sydney
Australia

A stamp.

Why didn't the skeleton go to the ball?

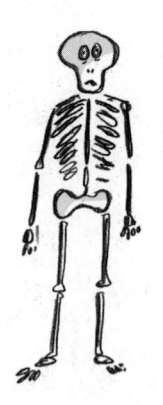

Because he had no body to dance with.

What's the difference between boogers and broccoli?

Kids won't eat broccoli.

What did one flea say to the other?

Shall we hop there or take the dog?

**What did the one tube
of glue say to the other?**

**"Let's stick
together."**

**I went to the doctor yesterday
and asked if she could do
anything for wind.**

**So she gave
me a kite.**

Why can't a nose be 12 inches long?

Because it would be a foot.

What do you take before every meal?

You take your seat.

Why did the scarecrow win a medal?

Because he was outstanding in his field.

What do you get when a chicken lays its eggs on the top of a hill?

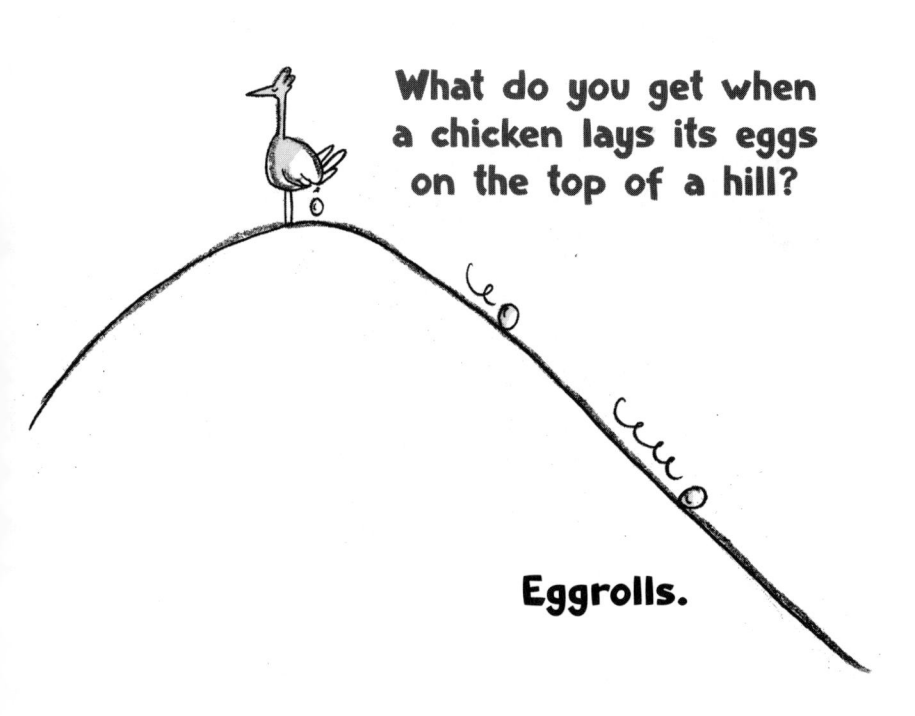

Eggrolls.

What did the cucumber
say to the vinegar?

"This is a fine
pickle you've got
us into!"

A chicken
crossing
the road . . .

is poultry
in motion.

It's difficult explaining puns
to kleptomaniacs.

They always take things, literally.

Why didn't the girl trust the ocean?

Because there was something fishy about it.

What do you call a dinosaur that's worried all the time?

A nervous rex.

Why did the girl drop the clock out the window?

Because she wanted to see time fly.

What starts with E, ends with E, and has only one letter in it?

Envelope.

What is a bat's motto?

Hang in there.

What do you get when you cross a comedian with crochet?

A knit wit.

How do cats end a fight?

They hiss and make up.

What do you call
a man who rolls
around in leaves?

Russell.

What's black and
smells like red paint?

Black paint.

What do you
call a Roman
emperor when he
catches a cold?

Julius Sneezer.

Where should
you leave your dog
when you go shopping?

In the
barking lot.

What do you give
an elephant with
big feet?

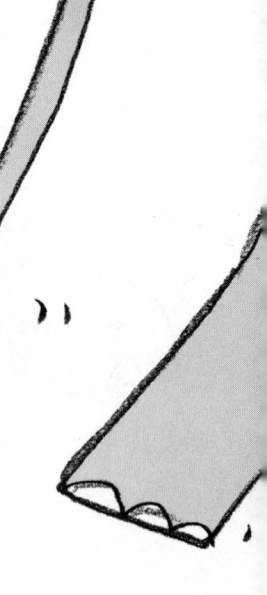

Lots of space.

What do cats
call mice?

Delicious.

Why did the
baker stop
making
donuts?

He got tired
of the hole
thing.

What do you get when you cross a cow with an earthquake?

A milkshake.

How do you toast a sheep?

"Here's to ewe!"

**Why did the computer
cross the road?**

To get a byte to eat.

**What do you call a robot that
always takes the longest route?**

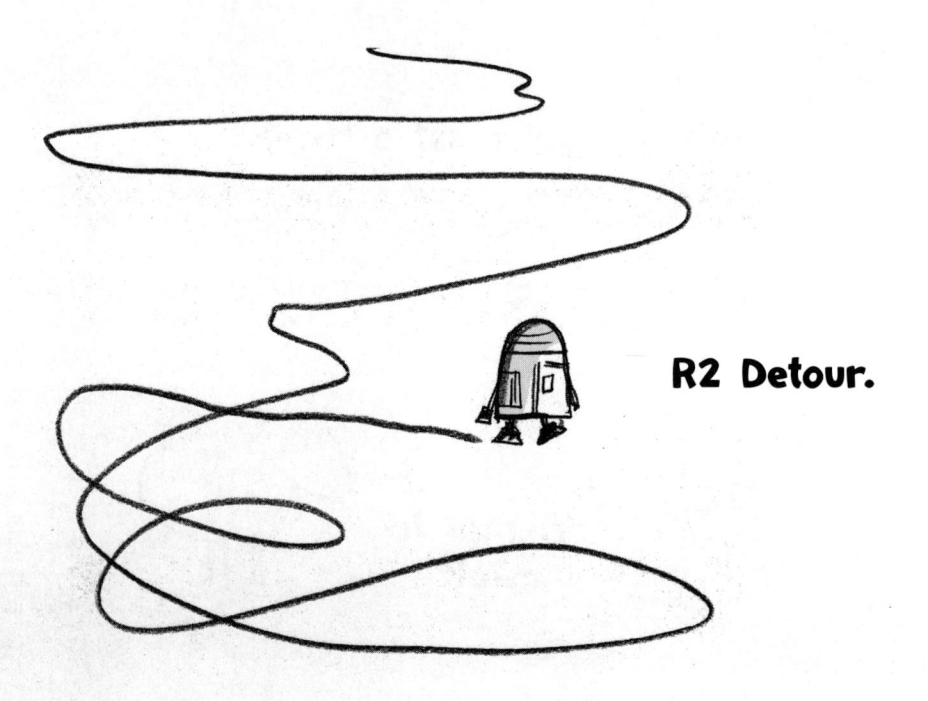

R2 Detour.

What do you call
a chicken with
lettuce in its eye?

Chicken caesar
salad.

What did the sushi say to the bee?

WASABI!

**What has one horn
and gives milk?**

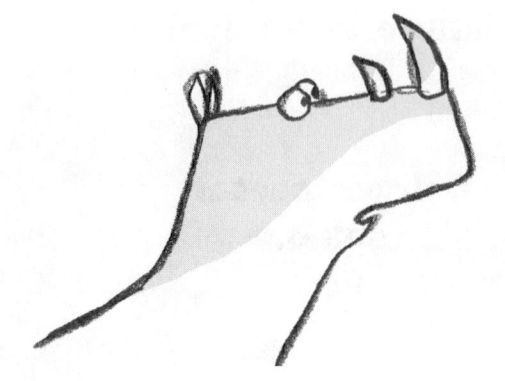

A milk truck.

How did the fisherman go deaf?

He lost his herring.

How do you catch a squirrel?

Climb a tree and act like a nut.

What did the policemen do with the hamburger?

They gave him a good grilling.

My friend keeps trying to convince me that he's a compulsive liar.

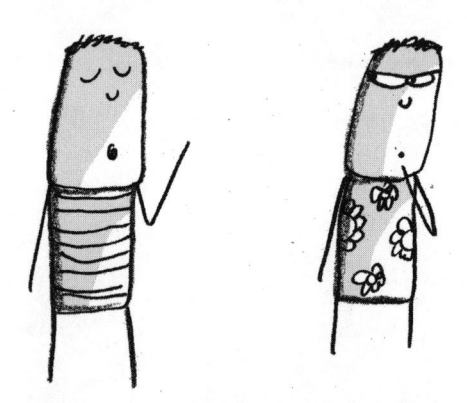

But I don't believe him.

Why did the house go to the doctor?

Because it had a window pane.

What happens to astronauts who misbehave?

They're grounded.

On the other hand . . .

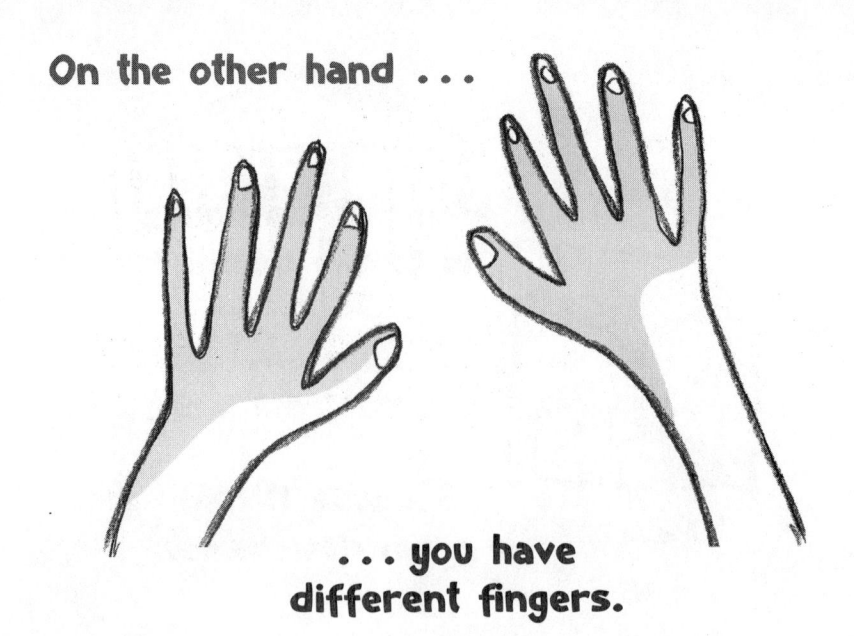

. . . you have
different fingers.

This is my
step ladder.

I never knew my
biological ladder.

Don't you hate it
when someone
answers their own
questions?

I do.

I, for one, like
Roman numerals.

My wife just found out I replaced
our bed with a trampoline.

She hit the roof.

I told my doctor that I broke
my arm in two places.

She told me to
stop going to
those places.

Knock Knock.

Who's there?

Knock.

Knock who?

Knock Knock.

Bacon and eggs walk into
a cafe and order some sodas.

The waiter says, "Sorry,
we don't serve breakfast."

I really must get rid of
my vacuum cleaner.

It's just
gathering dust.

What do religious rabbits say before they eat?

"Lettuce pray."

Where do you find a cow with no legs?

Right where you left it.

Exaggerations went up by a million percent last year.

How do you count cows?

With a cowculator.

What do you call a boomerang that doesn't come back?

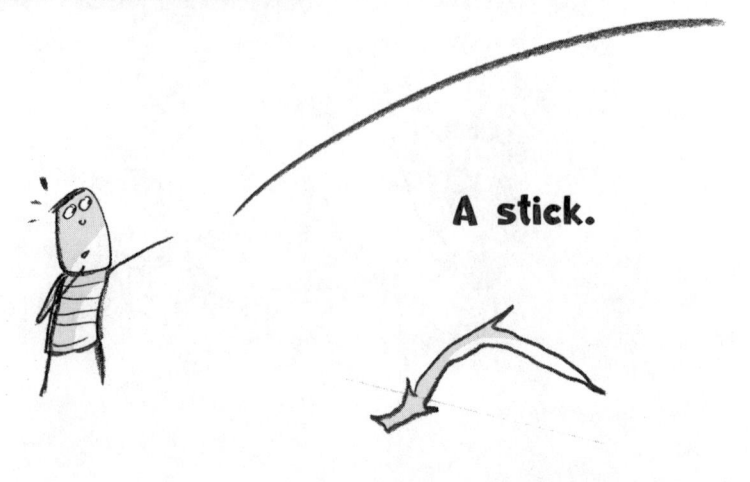

A stick.

Two antennas met on a roof, fell in love, and got married.

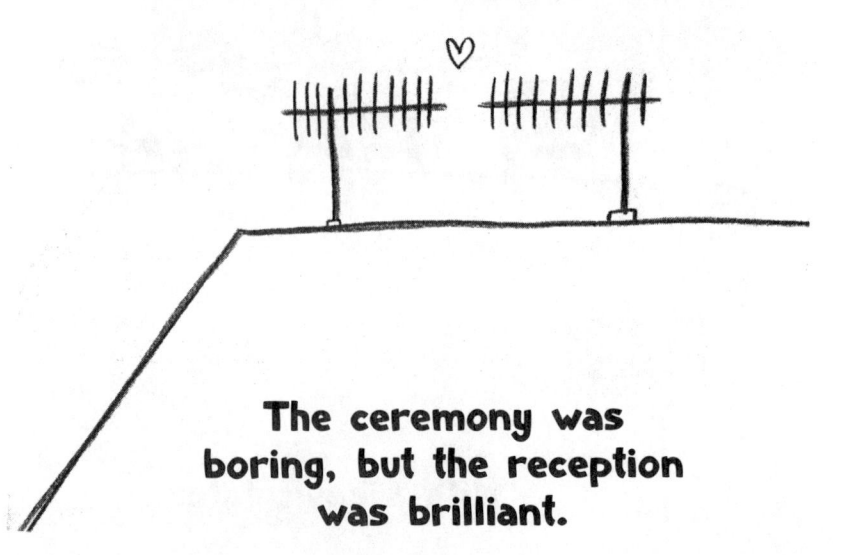

The ceremony was boring, but the reception was brilliant.

What occurs once in a minute, twice in a moment, but never in a decade?

The letter "m."

The grammar teacher was very logical.

He had a lot of comma sense.

Did you hear about the really rich rabbit?

He was a millionhare.

Why are hairdressers never late for work?

They know all the short cuts.

What is the color of the wind?

Blew.

Where does a sheep go
for a haircut?

To the baaa baaa shop.

How much room is needed for
fungi to grow?

As mushroom
as possible.

How do you know carrots
are good for your eyes?

Have you ever
seen a rabbit
wearing glasses?

Have you heard
about corduroy
pillows?

They're making
headlines.

Knock knock.

Who's there?

Beats.

Beats who?

Beats me.

What's an elephant's favorite vegetable?

Squash.

Two penguins walk into a bar . . .

which is stupid, because the second one really should have seen it.

Where do cows go for entertainment?

To the moo-vies.

What do you get when you cross a parrot and a centipede?

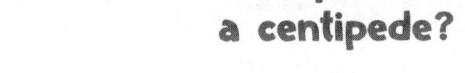

A walkie-talkie.

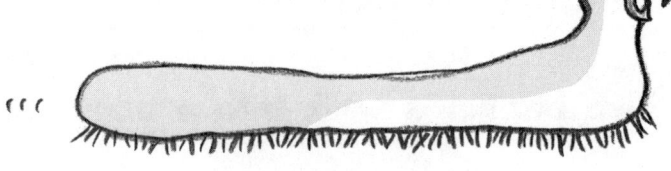

Do you want to hear a bad cat joke?

Just kitten.

What is a rabbit's favorite dance style?

Hip-Hop.

What do you call a ghost's mom and dad?

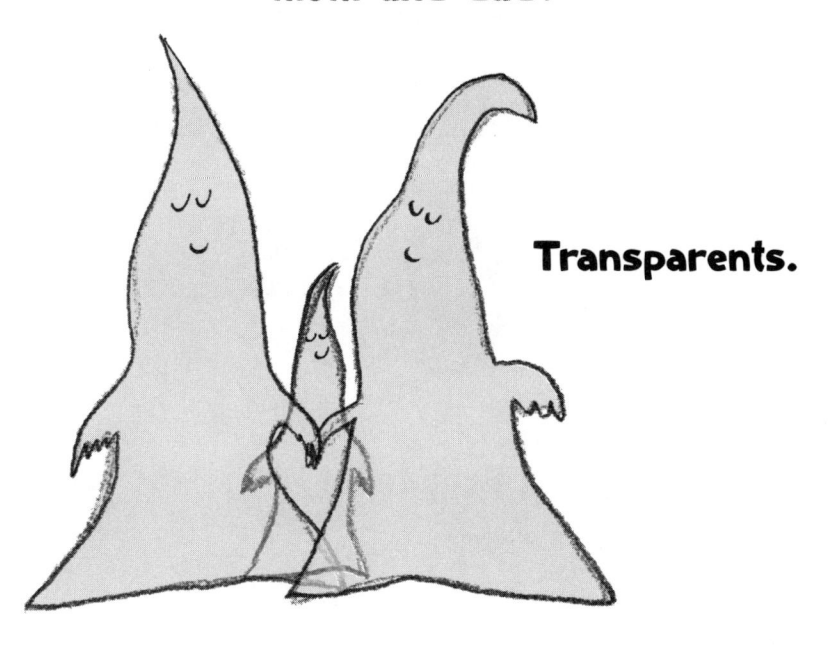

Transparents.

What do you call a bear in a phone booth?

Stuck.

What does the man in the moon do when his hair gets too long?

Eclipse it!

Why did the chicken
cross the road?

To hunt somebody down.

Knock knock!

Who's there?

The chicken.

What's the difference between a weird rabbit and a sporty rabbit?

One's a bit funny, the other's a fit bunny.

What did the cat say when she lost all her money?

"I'm paw!"

"This is your captain speaking."

"AND THIS IS YOUR CAPTAIN SHOUTING."

Where do you find giant snails?

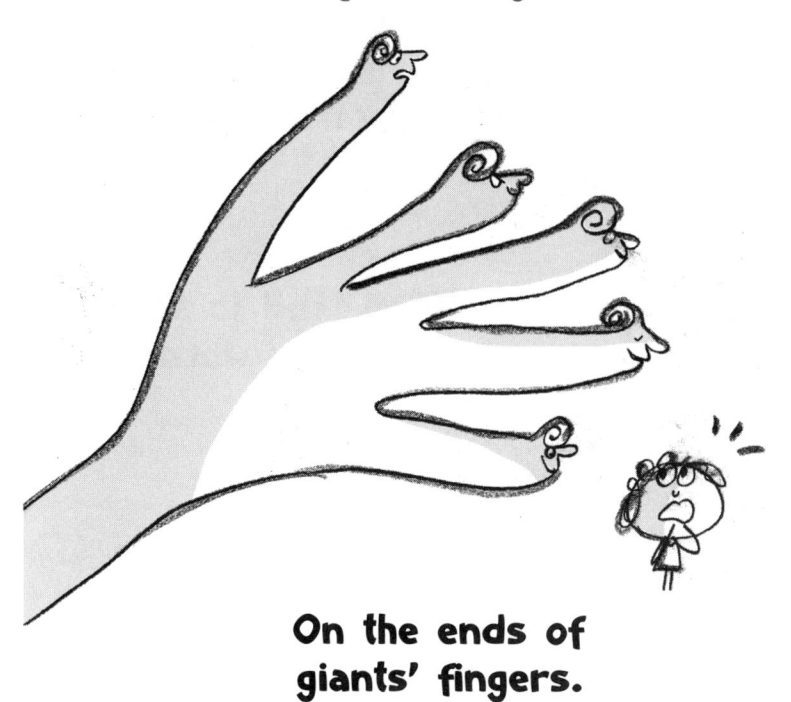

On the ends of giants' fingers.

Yesterday I held the door open for a clown.

I thought it was a nice jester.

You can always
trust a glue
salesman.

They tend to stick
to their word.

I didn't realize my dad was
a construction site thief.

But when I got home, all
the signs were there.

Can February march?

No, but
April may.

What starts with a P, ends
with an E, and has ten
thousand letters in it?

A post
office.

I really wanted
a camouflage shirt . . .

but I couldn't find one.

"I stand
corrected,"

. . . said the man in the
orthopedic shoes.

What swims and starts with a T?

Two ducks.

What's orange and sounds like a parrot?

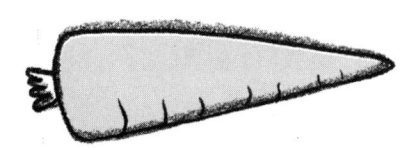

A carrot.

Have I told you the deja vu joke before?

The past, present, and future
walk into a bar.

It was tense.

What did the farmer say when he
couldn't find his tractor?

"Where's my
tractor?"

How many cats can you put
into an empty box?

Only one. After that,
the box isn't empty.

I feel sorry for that calendar.

Its days are
numbered.

What's brown and
sticky?

A stick.

Why did the two fours skip lunch?

They already 8.

Why did the can crusher quit his job?

Because it was soda pressing.

How much did the pirate pay for his hook and peg?

An arm and a leg.

**What do you call
a crocodile with GPS?**

A navi-gator.

**How can you drop a raw egg onto
a cement floor without cracking it?**

**Any way you want.
Cement floors are very hard to crack.**

What color is a burp?

Burple.

Why did the toilet paper go downstairs?

To get to the bottom.

**What side of a
sheep has the
most wool?**

The outside.

**What is heavy
forward but not
backward?**

Ton.

**Did you hear about the two bedbugs
who met in the mattress?**

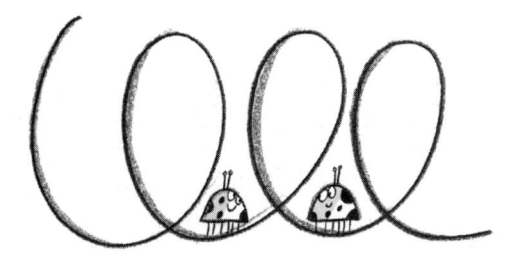

They got married in the spring.

What's the dream of every cow?

To go to the mooooo-n.

What's the difference between roast beef and pea soup?

You can roast beef, but you can't pea soup.

How did the
dinosaur know we
were coming?

The bronto-saw-us.

What accidents happen
every 24 hours?

Day breaks

and night falls.

I was struggling
to figure out how
lightning works.

Then it struck me.

"Nostalgia just isn't
what it used to be . . ."

Why is it impossible for a leopard to hide?

Because he will always be spotted.

What can be served but never eaten?

A tennis ball.

What type of dance do plumbers love?

Tap dance.

I was hoping to win the suntanning Olympics . . .

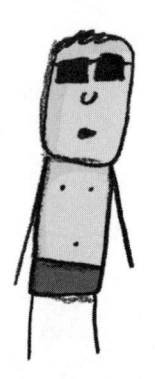

. . . but I only got bronze.

Why did the banana go to the doctor?

It wasn't peeling well.

What do you get if you eat pasta when you have a cold?

Macaroni sneeze.

What fruit keeps
teasing people?

The ba-na-na-na-na-na.

When is it best to
buy a chick?

**When it's
going cheep.**

Why is a bird more
talented than a fly?

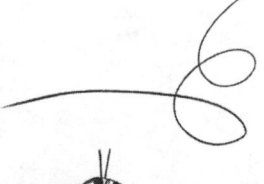

**A bird can fly
but a fly can't bird.**

What lives in the ocean and is
good for public transport?

An octobus.

I tried to sue
the airport for
misplacing my bags.

I lost
the case.

Why did the octopus beat the shark in a fight?

Because the octopus was well armed.

How do you make 7 an even number?

Get rid of the S.

Which is the best season for jumping on trampolines?

Spring.

What starts with a T, ends with a T, and is full of T?

A teapot.

Why did the sheep keep going down the road?

There were no ewe-turns allowed.

What did the stamp say to the envelope?

Roger Lightbottom
1001 Crocolide Blvd
Paris
07050, France

"Stick with me and we'll go places."

Where do sharks come from?

Finland.

What's a pirate's favorite hobby?

Ahrrrrt.

What happened when the semicolon broke the grammar laws?

It was given two consecutive sentences.

Why should you never get into a fight with 1, 3, 5, 7, and 9?

Because the odds will be against you.

What kind of songs do planets sing?

Nep-tunes.

How does a cat get what it wants?

 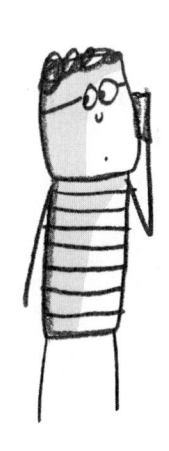

With gentle purr-suasion.

What do you call five giraffes?

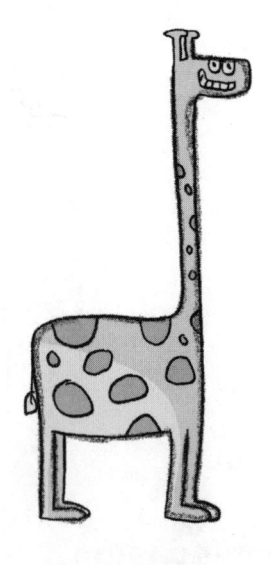

A high five.

What do ghosts use to wash their hair?

Sham-boo!

Which city never stays in the same place for long?

Rome.

Why would you put sugar under your pillow?

So that you have sweet dreams.

What is the worst kind of cat to have?

A cat-astrophe.

WOULD YOU RATHER...

Take a Shower

Stop that!

...or Shake a Tower?

What did mama cow
say to little cow?

"It's pasture bedtime."

What's big, white,
and lives on Mars?

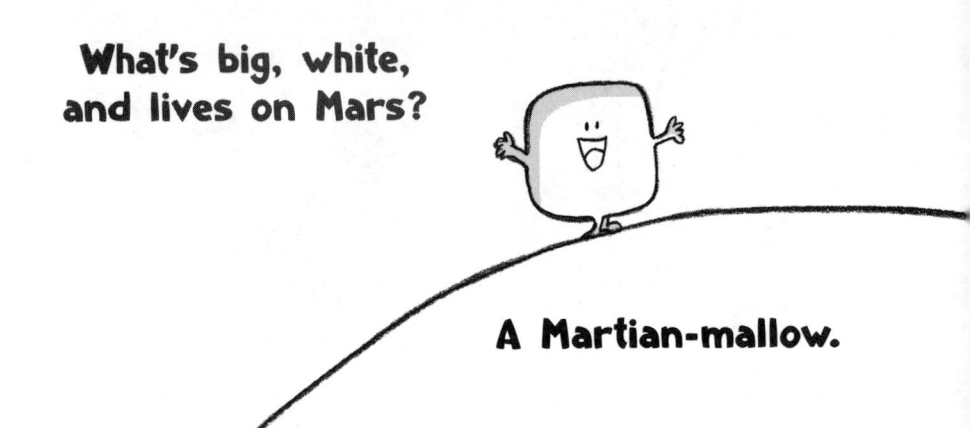

A Martian-mallow.

What's the most
tired part of a car?

The exhaust pipe.

How do whales cry?

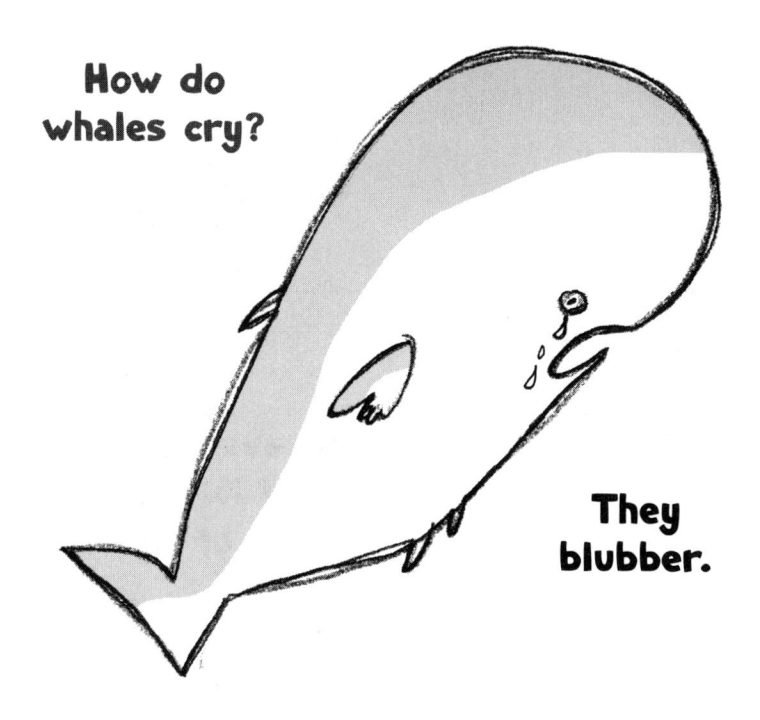

They blubber.

What do you call 2 octopi that look exactly the same?

Itentacle.

Why did the girl eat her homework?

Because her teacher said it was a piece of cake.

Finally they're making a film about clocks.

It's about time.

Have you heard the joke about the skunk?

Never mind, it really stinks.

What do you get when you cross fish and elephants?

Swimming trunks.

Why didn't the young pirate go to the movie?

Because it was ahrrr-rated.

What do you call two birds in love?

Tweethearts.

Why shouldn't you bring a chicken to school?

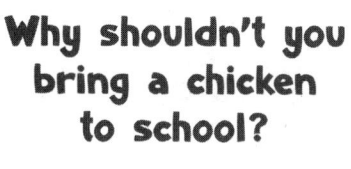

It might use fowl language.

Why did the cabinet go to the psychiatrist?

Because it kept talking to its shelf.

What did the one raindrop say to the other?

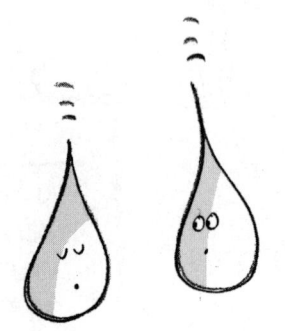

"Two's company, three's a cloud."

What's green and fuzzy and if it fell out of a tree would hurt you?

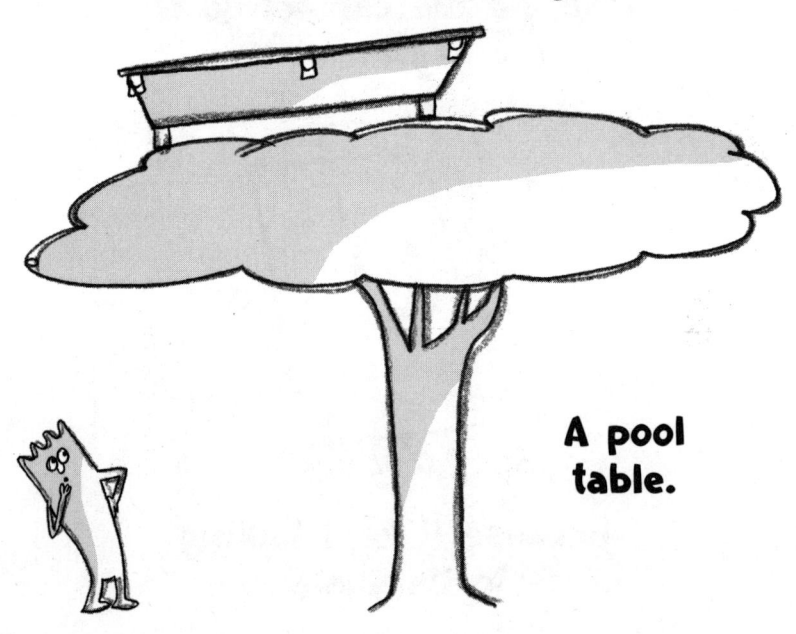

A pool table.

Can a match box?

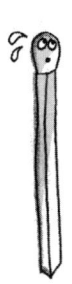 

No, but a tin can.

What do you get from a pampered cow?

Spoiled milk.

Why do pirates take ages to learn the alphabet?

Because they spend years at C.

Why didn't the pig get invited to any parties?

Because he was a boar.

How do you get a square root?

Plant a tree in a square pot.

What has four eyes but can't see?

Mississippi.

How did Dracula feel when he ate a sheep?

Baaaaaaaad.

I'm marrying a pencil.

I can't wait to introduce my parents to my bride 2B.

What's black and white and eats like a horse?

A zebra.

Did you know that 3.14
of sailors are . . .

Pi-rates.

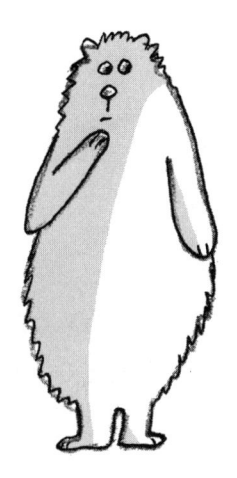

Why didn't
the bear go to
college?

Because bears
don't go to
college.

How do trees use their email accounts?

They just log in.

Why do cows have hooves instead of feet?

Because they lactose.

How can you tell if there's an elephant in your sandwich?

It's too heavy to lift.

Where do ghosts go swimming?

Lake Eerie.

What do you call a group of rabbits walking backward?

A receding hare line.

Why are mountain ranges funny?

Because they are hill-areas.

WOULD YOU RATHER...

Carry
a Mat

...or Marry
a Cat?

Why are mummies so vain?

Because they're all wrapped up in themselves.

What bread has the worst attitude?

Sourdough.

How do you make a glass of milkshake?

Give it a fright.

English can be
a complicated
language to learn.

**It can be understood through tough,
thorough thought, though.**

**What happens when dinosaurs
drive cars too fast?**

Tyrannosaurus wrecks.

Why did it take him 4 hours to finish the 20 page book?

Because he wasn't very hungry.

What kind of road do ghosts like?

Dead ends.

Why did the cat put the letter M into the freezer?

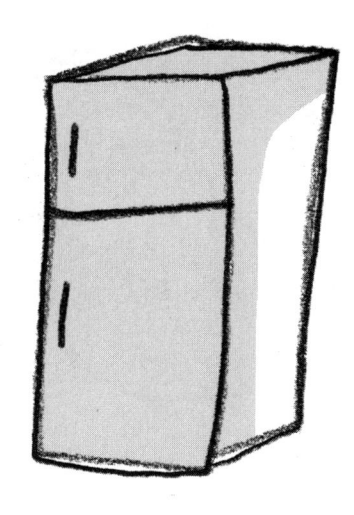

Because it turns ice into Mice.

What did the couch say while climbing Everest?

"Sofa, so good."

What do you get when you cross a snowman with a vampire?

Frostbite.

What do you call a napping bull?

A bulldozer.

What happens when you throw a blue pebble into the Red Sea?

It gets wet.

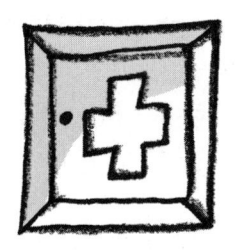

Why did the boy tip-toe past the medicine cupboard?

Because he didn't want to wake the sleeping pills.

Which driver will never get a parking ticket?

A screwdriver.

What did the rude triangle say to the circle?

"You're pointless!"

Why was the man fired from the calendar factory?

He took a day off.

What do you say when you throw a clock in the air?

"Time's up!"

How did Benjamin Franklin feel about discovering electricity?

He was totally shocked.

Why did H feel lost and alone?

NOWHERE

**Because he was in the
middle of nowhere.**

**What's the coldest
tropical island?**

Brrrrrrrr-muda.

Why did the invisible man decide not to take the job?

He just couldn't see himself doing it.

What did the table say to the chair?

"Dinner's on me."

What's the capital of California?

C.

What do you call it when a chicken stumbles as it crosses the road.

A road trip.

Why were they worried about the small bucket?

Because it was a little pail.

How do chickens dance?

Chick to chick.

What's a crocodile's favorite game?

Snap.

What kind of bow is impossible to tie?

A rainbow.

What do you call a dead fly?

A flew.

What kind of crazy creature lives on the moon?

A lunar tick.

**What happened
to the lost cattle?**

Nobody's herd.

**Did you hear about the ant
that was very smart?**

He was brilli-ant.

Why did the bicycle fall over?

Because it was two tired.

What do you call a cow who works for a gardener?

HERB'S
GARDENING
SERVICE

A lawn moo-er.

Why do dogs wag their tails?

Because no one else will do it for them.

What do you get if you put a family of ducks in a carton?

A box of quackers.

What do you call a cat with 8 legs that likes to swim?

An octopuss.

How do ghosts send letters abroad?

Scaremail.

What do you
call a cow in a
tornado?

A milkshake.

Why don't you ever
see hippos hiding in
trees?

Because they're very good at it.

What is white, has four ears, whiskers, and sixteen wheels?

Two bunnies on rollerblades.

What's a cat's favorite breakfast?

Mice Krispies.

What kind of music do balloons hate.

Pop!

Why did the boy eat the candle?

His mother told him to have a light snack.

Why did the girl study on top of the mountain?

She wanted a higher education.

What do aliens put their tea cups on?

Flying saucers.

What did the cat say to the dog?

"Check meow-t!"

If you eat 3/4ths of a pie, what do you get?

A stomachache.

What time is it when an elephant sits on your fence?

Time to get a new fence.

What kind of button can't be undone?

A belly button.

What has four legs and one head but only one foot?

A bed.

What type of cheese is made backward?

Edam.

What did the marmalade say to the bread?

"Stop loafing about!"

Why wouldn't the teddy bear eat anything?

He was already stuffed.

**Why did the
hamburger lose
the race?**

**It couldn't
ketchup.**

**What do you put in a barrel
to make it lighter?**

A hole.

**What did the one sock
say to the other sock in
the dryer?**

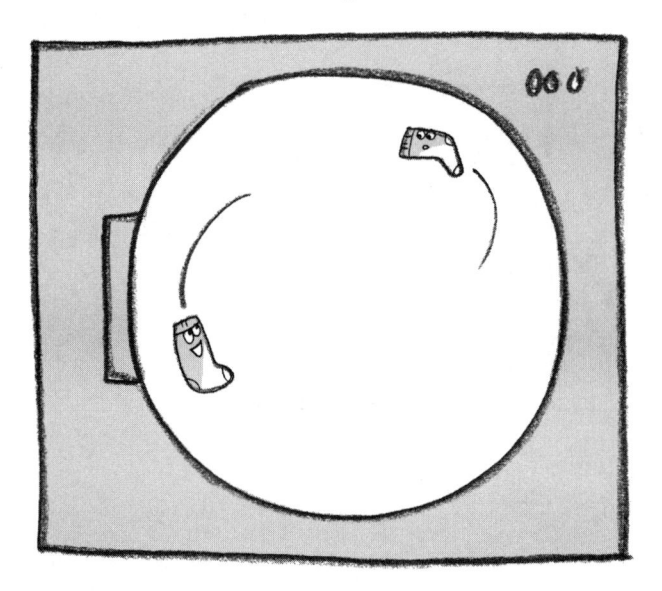

"See you next time round."

Why did the bug look away?

 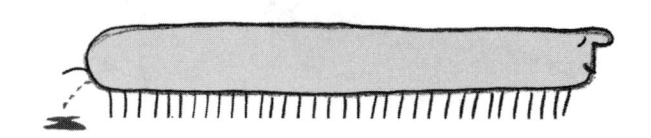

Because the centipede.

Why did the scientist remove the bell from her front door?

Because she wanted to win the no-bell prize.

What do you get when you cross a dinosaur with a pig?

Jurassic Pork.

Why did the watch go on vacation?

**He wanted
to unwind.**

**How do you make
a witch itch?**

You take away the W.

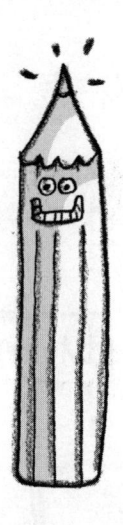

Why are riddles like pencils?

They're useless unless they've got a point.

Did you hear about the angry pancake?

It just flipped.

What do hedgehogs say when they kiss?

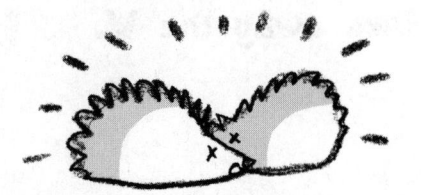

"Ouch!"

Who made the fish's wishes come true?

Its fairy codmother.

Where are cars most likely to get punctures?

At forks in the road.

What did the one eye say to the other?

"Between you and me, something smells."

Where do ghosts mail their letters?

At the ghost office.

What do you call a fish with no eye?

Fsh.

What name did the snail give to her shell?

Michelle.

What did the zero say to the eight?

"Nice belt."

What is a shark's favorite game?

Swallow the leader.

What did the one volcano say to the other?

"I lava you."

What do ants take
when they're ill?

Ant-ibiotics.

Where do animals go when
their tails fall off?

To the re-tail store.

What is a pig's
favorite ballet?

Swine Lake.

What has ears like
a cat, a tail like a cat,
but is not a cat?

A kitten.

What's pink and
fluffy?

Pink fluff.

What's blue and
fluffy?

Cold pink fluff.

What's the highlight of a cannibal wedding?

Toasting the happy couple!

What happened to the cat after it ate the clown fish?

It felt funny.

What belongs to you but others use more?

Hi, Steve.

Your name.

Don't trust stairs!

They're always up to something.

**What's worse
than a worm in
your apple?**

**Half a worm
in your apple!**

**What do you get when you cross a
ghost and a cat?**

A scaredy cat.

Why are dogs such
weird dancers?

Because they have two left feet.

What goes ha, ha, ha, ha, ha plonk?

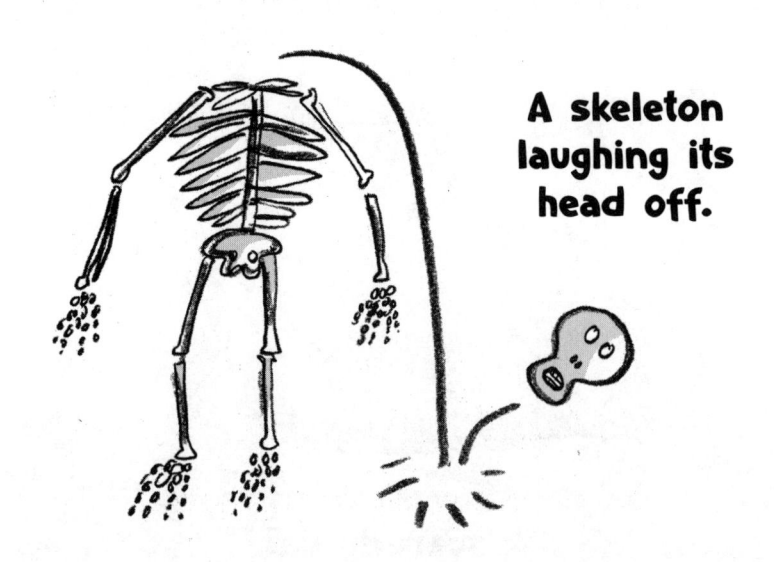

A skeleton
laughing its
head off.

What can you carry even though it weighs over 150 pounds?

A scale.

What's gray but turns red?

An embarrassed elephant.

**When does the
moon burp?**

When it's full.

**When is it bad luck to be
followed by a black cat?**

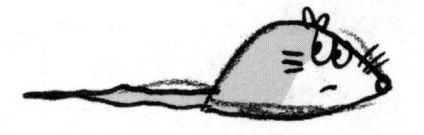

**When you're
a mouse.**

Why should you always take a pencil to bed?

To draw the curtains.

What has 4 legs and goes, "Oom, oom"?

A backward cow.

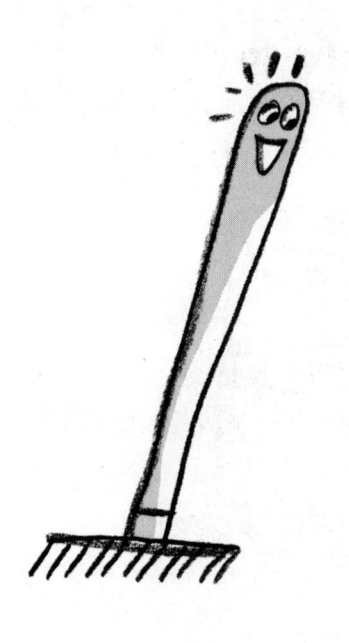

Why was the rake so
excited about
the future?

Because it was
about to turn over
a new leaf.

Where do letters sleep?

In an alpha-bed.

Why is it so hard to fool a snake?

Because you can't pull its leg.

Why was the sheep itchy?

skritch
skritch

Because it had fleece.

What does 234y3x + 334y/547z
x 0.021(0.44) / y²99 and
z - 63/22 get you?

A headache.

**What do you call a
bird that's been eaten
by a cat?**

A swallow.

**Why did the crab
never share?**

**Because he was
shellfish.**

What happened to the Dalmatian that fell into the washing machine?

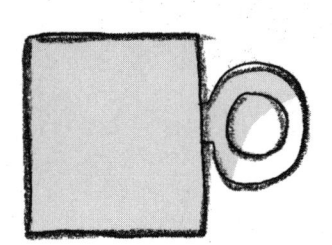 

It came out spotless.

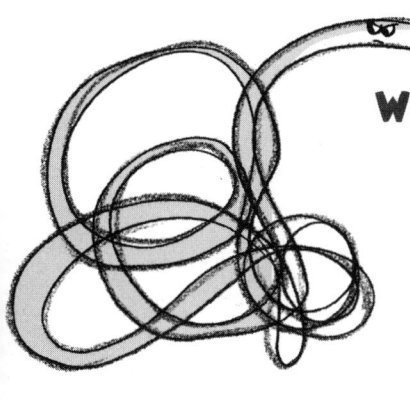

What did the rope say after it got tangled?

"Oh no, knot again!"

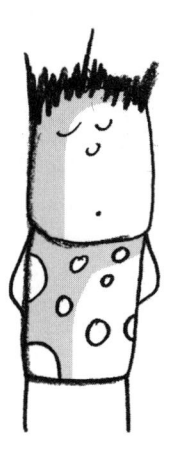

I entered a joke-writing competition ten times and hoped I'd win.

Sadly, no pun in ten did.

Why did the lady divorce the grape?

Because she was tired of raisin' kids.

What did the one ghost ask the other?

"Do you believe in humans?"

How did the man cut the sea in half?

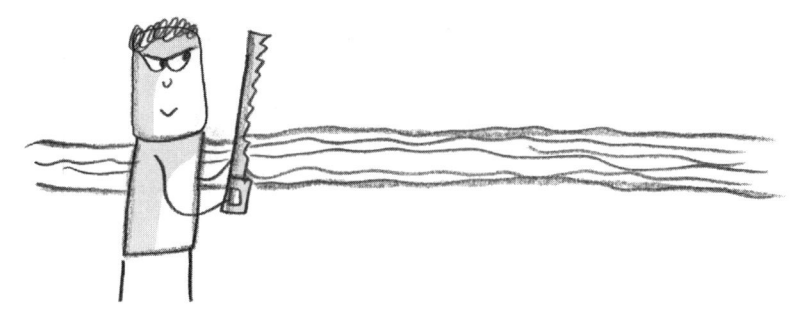

With a sea saw.

What happened to the monster that swallowed an electricity generator?

It was in shock for a month.

Where do birds invest their savings?

In the stork market.

How does a mouse feel just after it's taken a shower?

Squeaky clean.

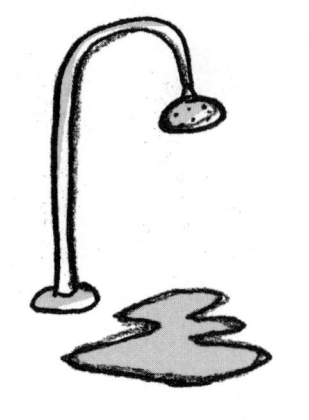

Why did the cannibal eat his mother's sister?

Because he was an aunt-eater.

What does a ball do when it stops rolling?

Looks round.

Why are frogs so happy?

Because they just eat whatever bugs them.

What's the difference between a greyhound and a duck?

One goes quick and the other goes quack.

What is the longest word?

SMILES.

Because it has a mile between
the first and last letters.

When do elephants
have eight legs?

When there are two elephants.

What runs but doesn't get anywhere?

A fridge.

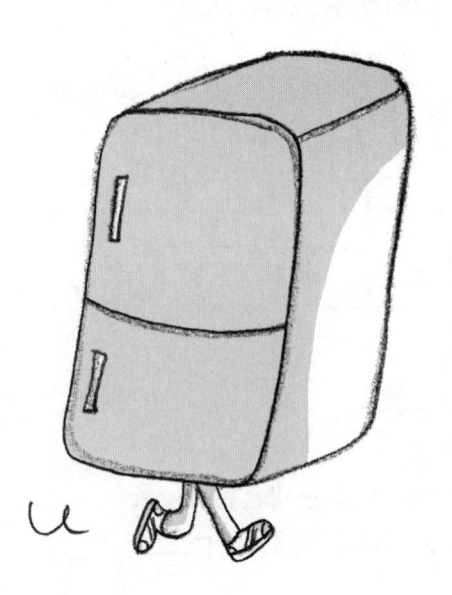

What do cows like to dance to?

Any kind of moosic.

Why do birds fly south for the winter?

SOUTH

It's easier than walking.

Why do pandas like old movies?

CASA BLANCA

Because they're black and white.

What do witches race on?

Vroom sticks.

How do you prepare for an astronaut's birthday?

Planet.

What does a cat say when you step on its tail?

"Me-ow!"

What did the tie
say to the hat?

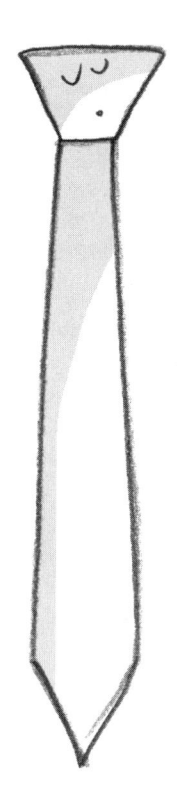

"You go on ahead.
I'll hang around."

Why can you never trust atoms?

Because they
make up
everything.

WOULD YOU RATHER...

Sleep in a Bed?

beep
beep

beep

...or
Beep in a Sled?

What do you call an overweight dog?

A round hound.

What kind of ant is good with numbers?

An account-ant.

I'm reading a book about anti-gravity.

It's impossible to put down.

**What do you get
when you mix a
banana with a bus?**

A fruit that can seat 36 people.

**What's the
noisiest sport?**

**Tennis, because
there's always a racket
on the court.**

How do cats eat spaghetti?

With their mouths, just like everyone else.

Why do the French eat snails?

They don't like fast food.

What is a French cat's favorite dessert?

Chocolate mouse.

What do you call a sad strawberry?

A blueberry.

What is the loudest kind of pet?

A trumpet.

On what day
of the week do
chickens hide?

Fry-day.

What do you get if you cross
some ants with some ticks?

All kinds
of crazy
antics.

Why did the nurse go to art school?

To learn to draw blood.

How do you get straight As?

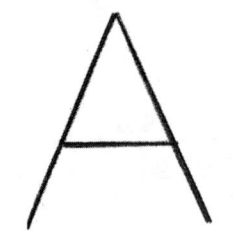

Use a ruler.

What do you get when you whisk milk, butter, sugar, and 100 eggs?

A very sore arm.

How can you tell an elephant
from a mouse?

**Try lifting it.
If you can't, it's an elephant.**

What do you call a
donkey with 3 legs?

A wonky.

What's the
difference
between legal
and illegal?

One's a sick bird.

What sport do
you play with a
wombat?

Wom.

Did you hear
about the guy
who invented
Lifesavers?

They say he
made a mint.

Who built King Arthur's round table?

Sir Cumference.

My mom bet me $100 I couldn't make a car from spaghetti.

You should have seen the look on her face as I drove pasta.

What's red and goes up and down?

A tomato in an elevator.

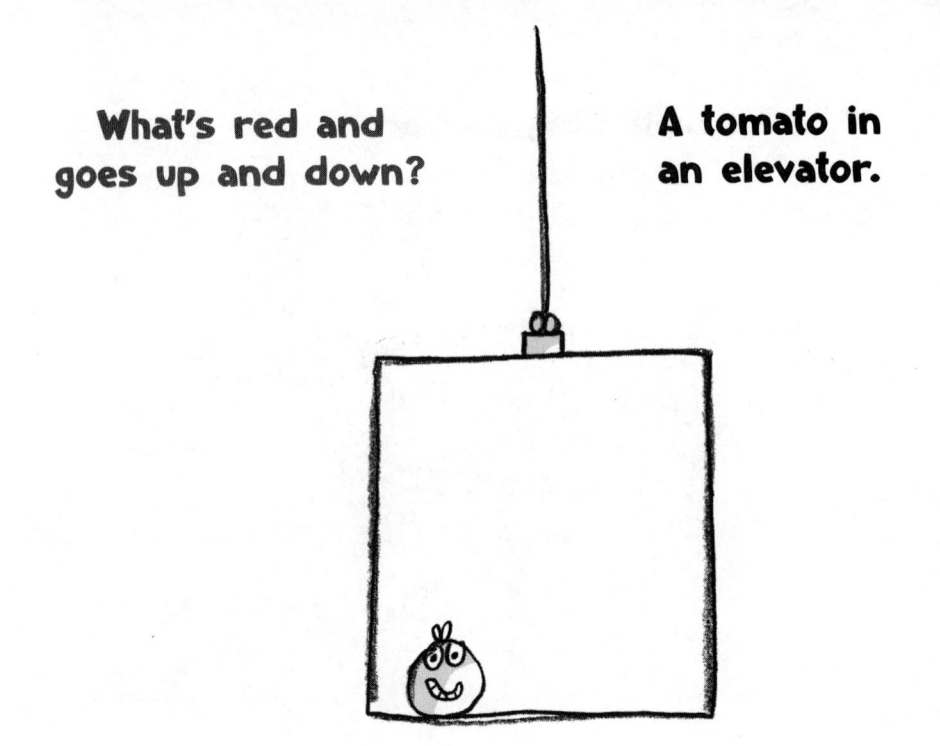

Why did the orange stop?

Because it ran out of juice.

What shoes are made from banana peels?

Slippers.

What is the best way to catch a fish?

Ask someone to throw it to you.

Where do ants go for dinner?

To the restaur-ant.

What happened after the cat ate a ball of wool?

She had mittens.

What do you call a factory that sells good products?

A satisfactory.

Why was the piano on
the porch?

Because it couldn't
find its keys.

I just heard
a joke about a
piece of paper.

It was tearable.

What do cows love to drink?

Smooooothies.

Where do you find an upside-down tortoise?

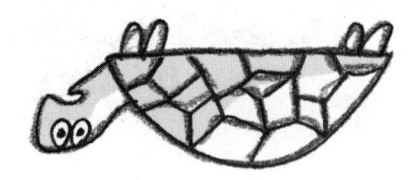

Right where you left it.

How did Thomas Edison invent the light bulb?

He got a bright idea.

What do rabbits use in the shower?

Hare conditioner.

What did the fog say to the boat?

I mist you.

Which country has lots
of dinnerware?

The United Plates of America.

What do you call two
bananas?

A pair of slippers.

What did the computer do to his foot when he lost his shoe?

He rebooted it.

What's a dog's favorite instrument?

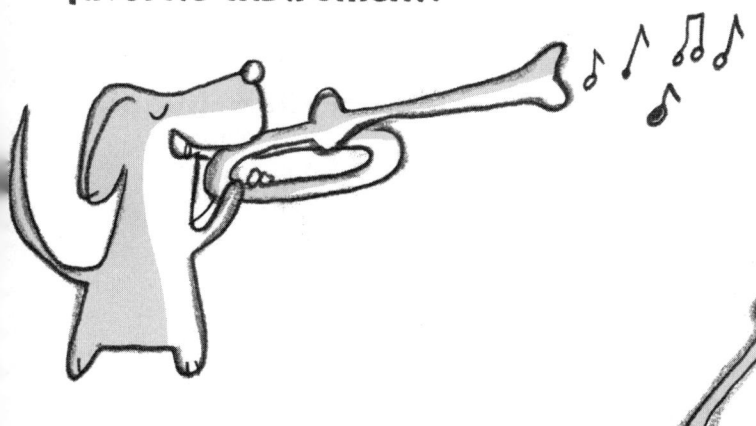

A trombone.

What was the bunny's favorite music?

Hip-hop.

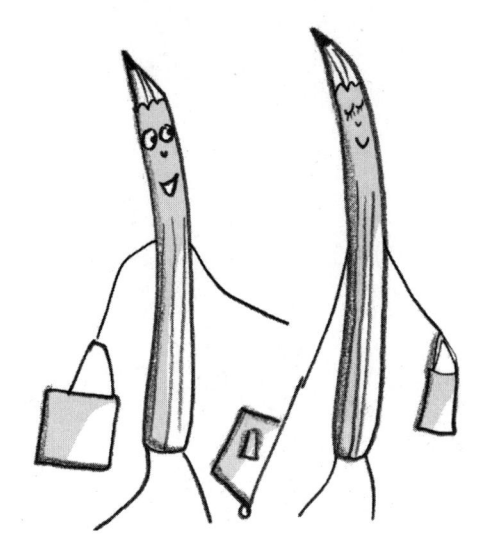

DEPARTURES

Where do pencils spend their vacations?

In Pencilvania.

What do you call a tired pea?

Sleep-pea.

What kind of key
opens a banana?

A monkey.

What lights up a
sports stadium?

A soccer match.

What happens to spoons that overwork?

They go stir-crazy.

I saw a kidnapping today.

I decided not to wake him up.

When a clown farts . . .

. . . does it smell funny?

If you ever need an ark . . .

. . . I Noah guy.

What do you call a
Frenchman in sandals?

Felippe Fallop.

He used to be a banker.

But then he lost interest.

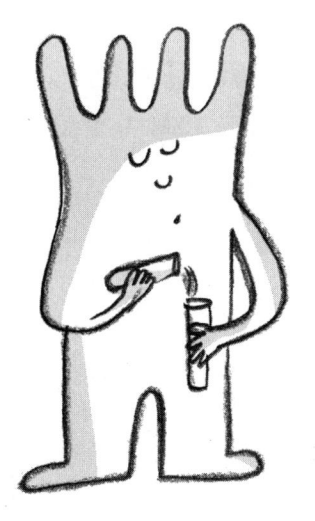

He told a bad
chemistry joke.

There was
no reaction.

Jokes about German sausages . . .

. . . really are the wurst!

What did the pirate say when he turned 80?

Aye matey.

Sometimes I tuck my knees into chest and lean forward.

It's just how I roll.

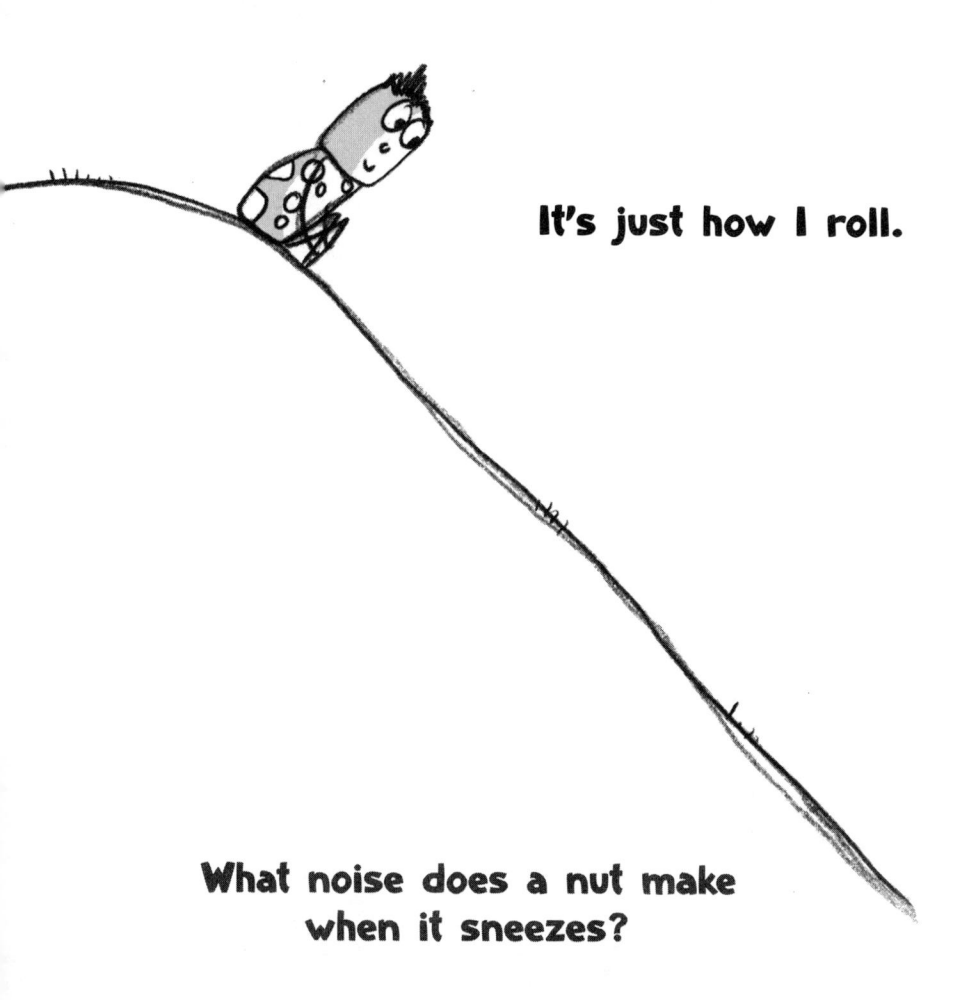

What noise does a nut make when it sneezes?

CASHEW!

What goes hahahahaHAHAhaha-THUMP?

A monster laughing his head off.

What kind of room can you eat?

A mushroom.

How do tuna and cod watch the news?

On telefishion.

Which is fastest, cold or heat?

Heat. Because you can catch a cold.

What was the dentist's favorite course in college?

Flossophy.

How does a monster count to 19?

On his fingers.

Doctor doctor, I haven't slept for days!

Why not?

Because I sleep at night.

What do you find in the middle of the ocean?

The letter "e."

Who delivers gifts to dogs on Christmas Eve?

Santa Paws.

She has an addiction to cheddar cheese . . .

. . . but it's only mild.

He used to be afraid
of hurdles . . .

. . . but he got over it.

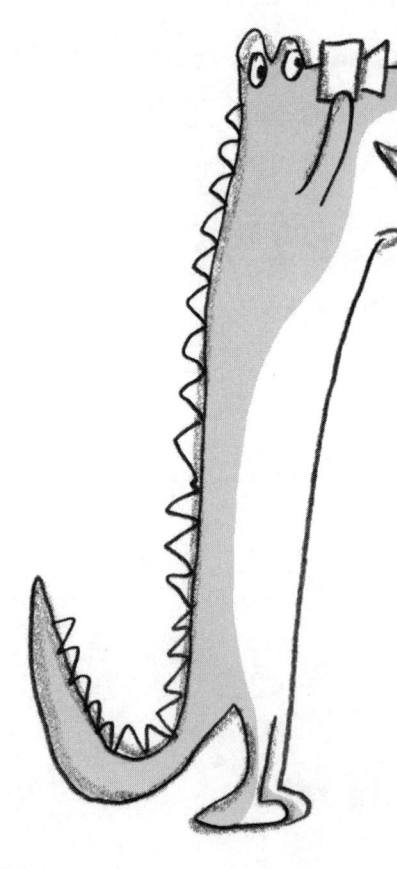

What do you call
a crocodile with
a new camera?

Happy snappy.

Murphy's Law says anything that can go wrong will go wrong.

Cole's Law is thinly sliced cabbage.

Coleslaw

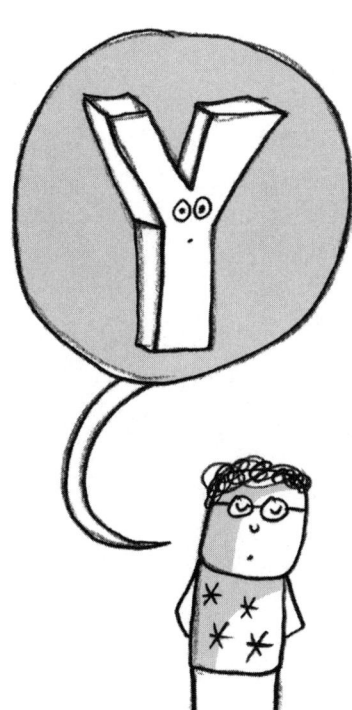

I'm friends with 25 letters of the alphabet.

I just don't know Y.

If you have 12 eggs in one hand
and 15 apples in the other,
what have you got?

Weirdly big
hands.

My brother recently got flattened
by a pile of books.

He's only got his shelf to blame.

Why does a milking stool only have three legs?

Because the cow has the udder.

What do you always get on your birthday?

Another year older.

**What do you call
a pack of wolves?**

Wolfgang.

Why do cats make great pets?

Because they are purrfect.

**What happened after the cat
ate the clown fish?**

It felt funny.

Why did the painting go to jail?

**Because it
was framed.**

What do you find on a very tiny beach?

Microwaves.

What did the scarf say to the hat?

**You go ahead,
I'll hang around.**

Did you hear about the magic tractor?

**It was just driving along and then
suddenly turned into a field!**

How do cats make coffee?

In a purrcolator.

What do trash collectors eat?

Junk food.

GARBAGE TRUCK

WACKDONALD'S

How did Cinderella's cat get to the ball?

With the help of her Furry Godmother.

What can you always count on?

Your fingers.

Why do rabbits have fur coats?

**Because they look silly
in leather jackets.**

How do you make antifreeze?

Send her to the North Pole!

When is the moon
not hungry?

When it's full.

What does a cat like to eat on a hot day?

A mice cream cone.

Why can't penguins fly?

Darn, still too expensive!

They can't afford the airplane tickets!

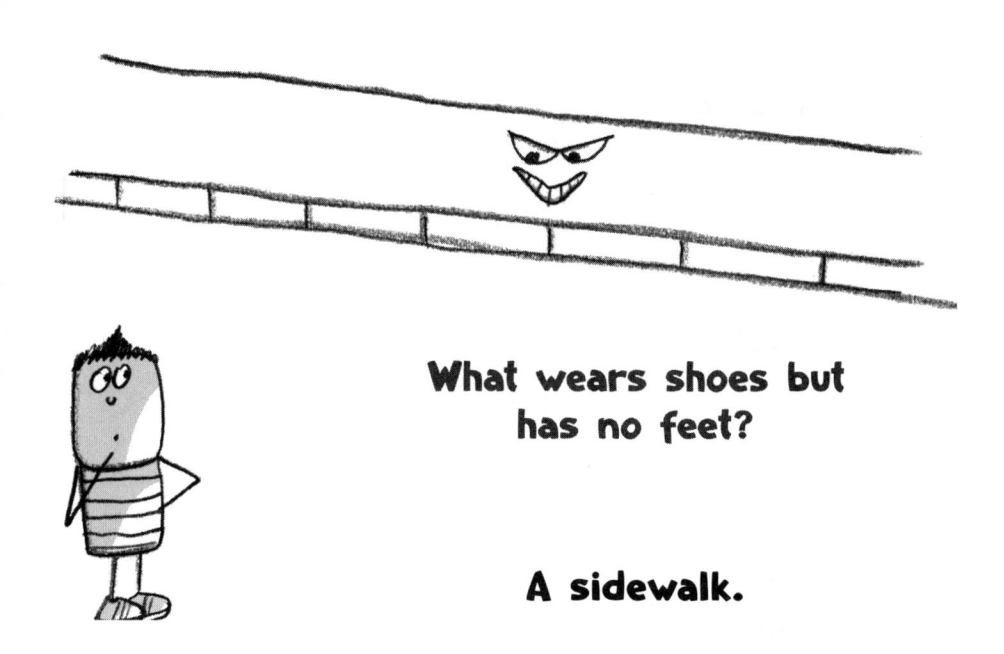

**What wears shoes but
has no feet?**

A sidewalk.

**What sort of stories does
a ship captain tell his children?**

Ferry tales.

What do you call a fish with four eyes?

Fiiiish.

What did the frog order for dinner?

A burger and Diet Croak.

What's big, gray, and drones on when it talks?

A mumbo jumbo.

blah de blah de blah de blah

What's hairy and sneezes?

A coconut with a cold.

ATCHOO!

What do the letter A and a rose have in common?

Bs come after them.

Why was the cat grouchy?

Bad mewd.

What sits on the seabed and shakes?

A nervous wreck.

How did the cow
transport all his stuff?

He rented a mooving truck.

How does a dog stop a movie?

He uses paws.

Why do mice need oiling?

SQuEAK
SQuEAK

Because they squeak.

How do you get rid of varnish?

Take away the R.

When is a door
not a door?

When it's ajar.

If you slice five peaches into five pieces, what do you end up with?

Sticky fingers.

What do you call a camel with three humps?

Humphrey.

How can you make
your money go a
long way?

Put your money in a rocket!

What did the policeman say when a spider crawled down his back?

You're under a vest!

What does a cat rest on at night?

A caterpillow.

How do chicks get out of their shells?

They eggs it.

What do you call a girl with a frog on her head?

Lily.

**Did you hear about the
lazy skeleton?**

He was bone idle.

What do you get if you cross an elephant with a mouse?

A huge hole in the baseboard!

Why was the glowworm disappointed?

The kids weren't all that bright.

What did one toilet say to the other?

You look a bit flushed.

How many police officers did it take to arrest a light bulb?

None. It turned itself in.

What's worse than raining cats and dogs?

Hailing taxis.

What do you get when the air-conditioning in a rabbit hole stops working?

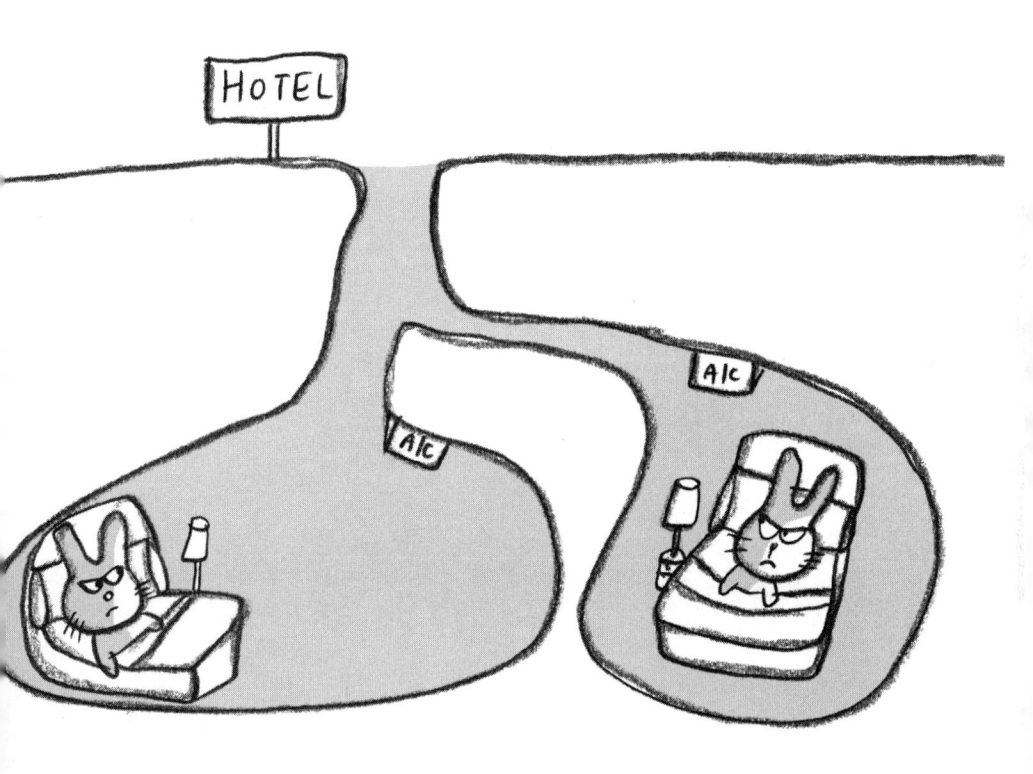

Hot cross bunnies.

What kind of cats are good at bowling?

Alley cats.

Why did Captain Hook cross the road?

To get to the second hand store.

How do you know carrots are good for your eyes?

Have you ever seen a rabbit with a flashlight?

Did you hear about the blacksmith dog?

When anyone shouts at him, he bolts for the door.

What's the difference between elephants and grapes?

Grapes are purple.

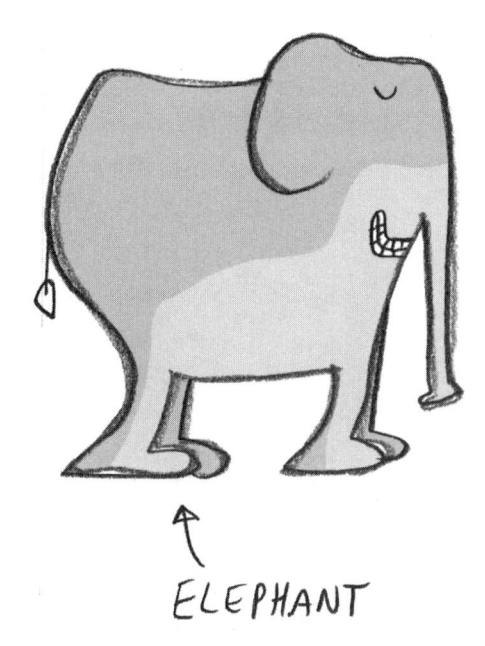

ELEPHANT

GRAPE

What's green and goes camping?

A brussels scout.

What is the shiniest fish in the sea?

A starfish.

He didn't like his beard at first . . .

. . . then it grew on him.

The boy gave away all his dead batteries.

Free of charge!

My dog Rover used to chase this kid on a bike a lot.

Eventually, I had to take Rover's bike away.

Why did the physics teacher break up with the biology teacher?

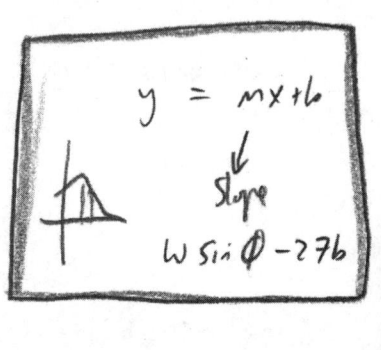

There was no chemistry.

If you know a really
good fish pun . . .

. . . please let
minnow.

How did the tree
feel in spring?

Releaved.

Why shouldn't you tell jokes about peanut butter?

People may spread it around.

What's the worst thing about a class on ancient history?

The teacher tends to Babylon.

When my wife asked me to stop
impersonating a flamingo . . .

. . . I really had
to put my foot
down.

What did Cinderella say when her
photos got lost in the mail?

One day my prints
will come . . .

Why did the sea urchin dream of space?

He wanted to be a starfish.

What's the best thing about elevator jokes?

They work on so many levels.

What do you call a boy named Lee who has no one to talk to?

Lonely.

Why do dragons sleep during the day?

So they can fight knights.

What do you get when you cross a snake with a pie?

A pie-thon.

Why should you stand in a corner if you're cold?

They're 90 degrees.

Did you hear about the mathematician who was afraid of negative numbers?

He'd stop at nothing to avoid them.

-3 -2 -1 0

Where do you learn to make banana splits?

At sundae school.

**What did the tree
say to the wind?**

Leaf me alone!

What do prisoners use to call each other?

Cell phones.

What never asks questions but is often answered?

A doorbell.

Why did the cantaloupe jump in the lake?

It wanted to be a watermelon.

What kind of insect is difficult to understand?

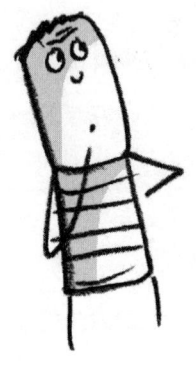

A mumblebee.

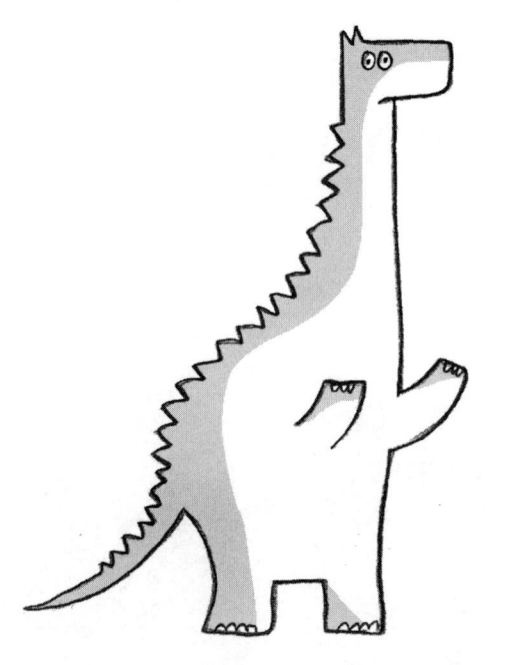

Why can't dinosaurs clap?

Because they're dead.

What's the difference between a school teacher and a train?

One says: "Spit that gum out!" And the other says: "Chew chew! Chew chew!"

What do you call a man with a spade in his head?

Doug.

What's the best time to eat a crispy apple?

At crunch time.

Where do fish keep their savings?

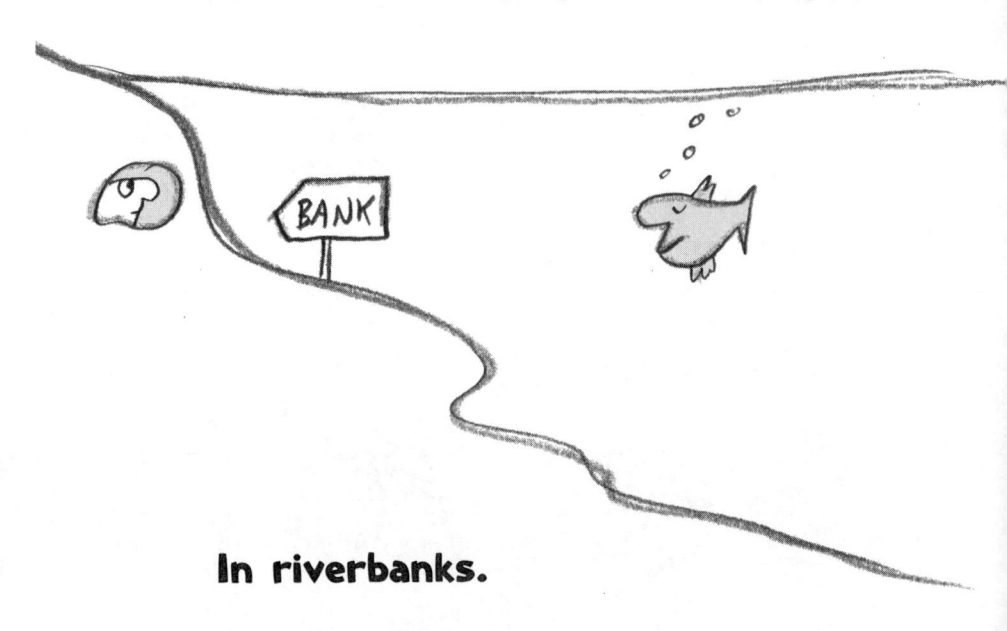

BANK

In riverbanks.

Where do you find Mexico?

On a map.

What do you call a one-legged giraffe?

Eileen.

Why was there thunder and lightning in the laboratory?

The scientists were brainstorming.

What's black, red, black, red,
black, red, black, red?

**A zebra with
a sunburn.**

Where do insects go shopping?

The flea market.

What did the one candle say to the other?

I'm going out tonight.

What do you call a funny mountain?

Hill-arious.

What goes through tunnels and over hills but doesn't move?

A road.

What did one penny say to the other?

We make cents.

Why do moon rocks taste better than earth rocks?

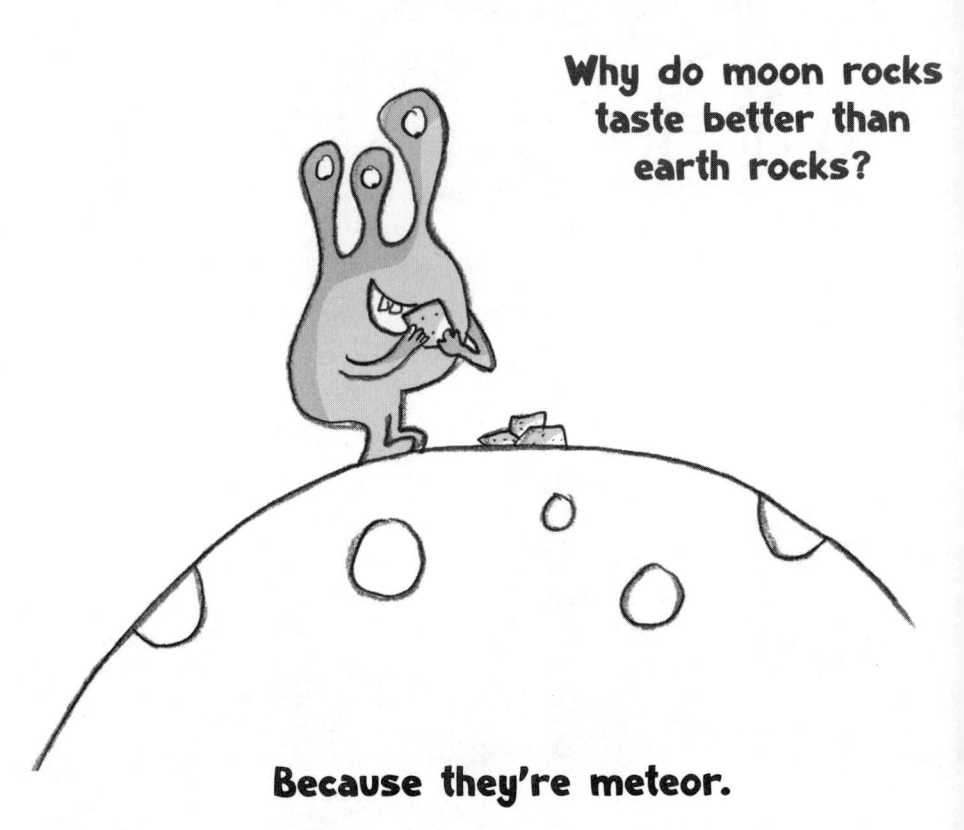

Because they're meteor.

Why was the man looking for food on his friend's head?

Because his friend had said: "Dinner's on me!"

Why is Peter Pan always flying?

Because he Neverlands.

Where do you find an upside-down tortoise?

Exactly where you left it.

What happened to the duck who heard a really funny joke?

He totally quacked up.

What snake is good at building houses?

A boa constructor.

What do you get when you mix a cow with a duck?

Milk and quackers.

Why did the man put his money in the freezer?

He wanted cold, hard cash.

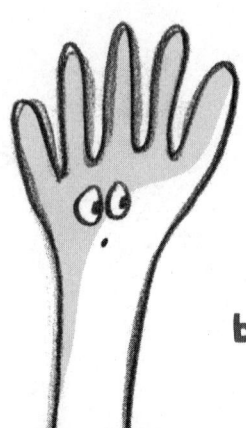
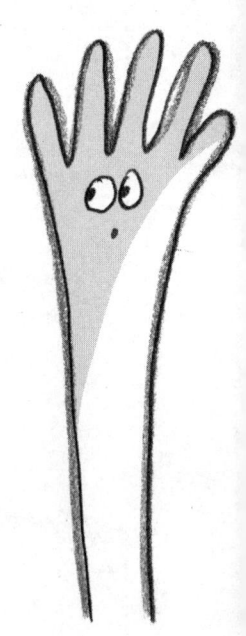

Which hand is it better to write with?

Neither, you should write with a pen!

Why did the man go out with a prune?

Because he couldn't find a date.

Why do you go to bed at night?

Because the bed won't come to you.

Were you long in hospital?

**No, I was the same size
as I am now.**

What's the difference between bird flu and swine flu?

One requires tweetment and the other needs oinkment.

What do you call helping a lemon in trouble?

Lemon-aid.

What's green and sits moping in the corner?

The Incredible Sulk.

I stayed up all night trying
to work out where the
sun was . . .

. . . then it dawned on me.

Where should a 400-pound alien go?

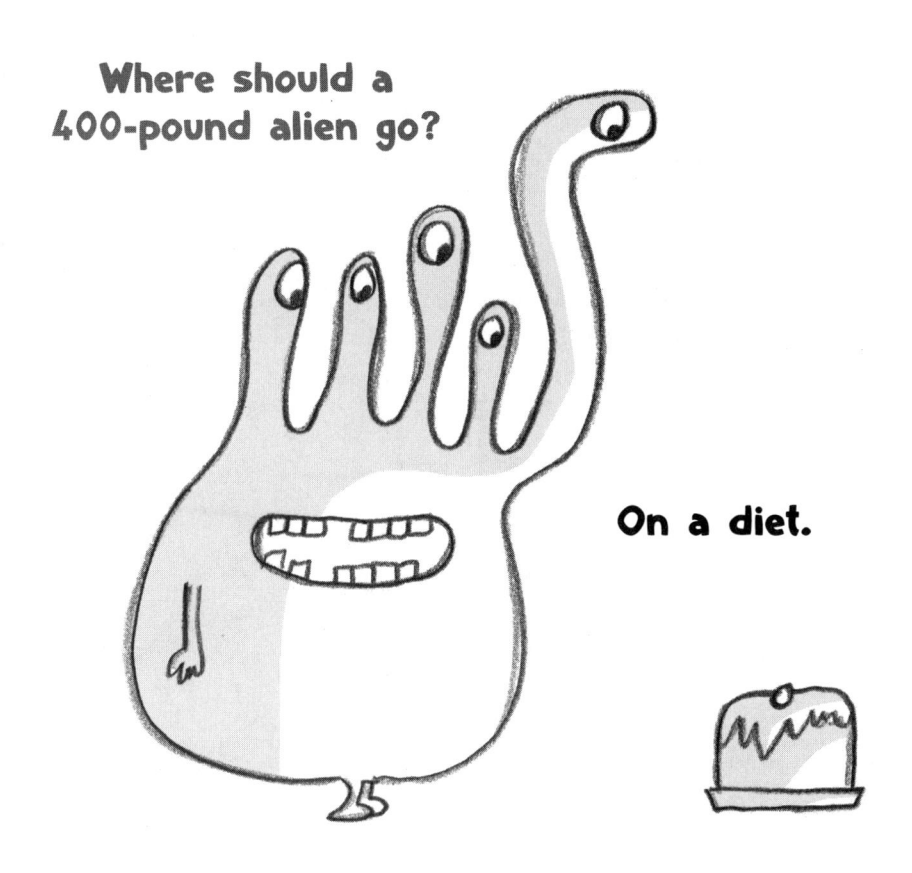

On a diet.

What did the mayonnaise say when the refrigerator door was opened?

Close the door, I'm dressing.

How do you get two whales in a car?

Start in England and head west.

Why do pelicans carry fish in their beaks?

Because they haven't got pockets.

What was the tree's favorite drink?

Root beer.

Why aren't koalas
actual bears?

They don't
have the right
koalafications.

Why was the drum so sleepy?

..YAWN

He was beat.

What kind of shoes does a ninja wear?

Sneakers.

What did the paper say to the pencil?

Write on!

What kind of dinosaur
makes a brilliant
English teacher?

A Thesaurus.

Why do eggs make such good fighter pilots?

Because they can scramble really fast.

I used to have terrible amnesia.

I used to have terrible amnesia.

How can you tell if there is an elephant under your bed?

You smack your head on the ceiling.

Where do werewolves live?

In warehouses.

What do you call a miserable ship?

A woe boat.

Why was the severely allergic woman worried about the weather?

Because it was raining cats and dogs.

Why didn't the cake like to play golf with the donut?

Because he always got a hole in one.

What has many thousands of ears but can't hear a thing?

A field of corn.

What musical instrument did the dentist love to play?

The tuba toothpaste.

Why was the oak tree going to the dentist?

To get a root canal.

Why are fish so smart?

Because they're always in a school.

Why are horses useless at dancing?

Because they have two left feet.

What's the difference between a television set and a newspaper?

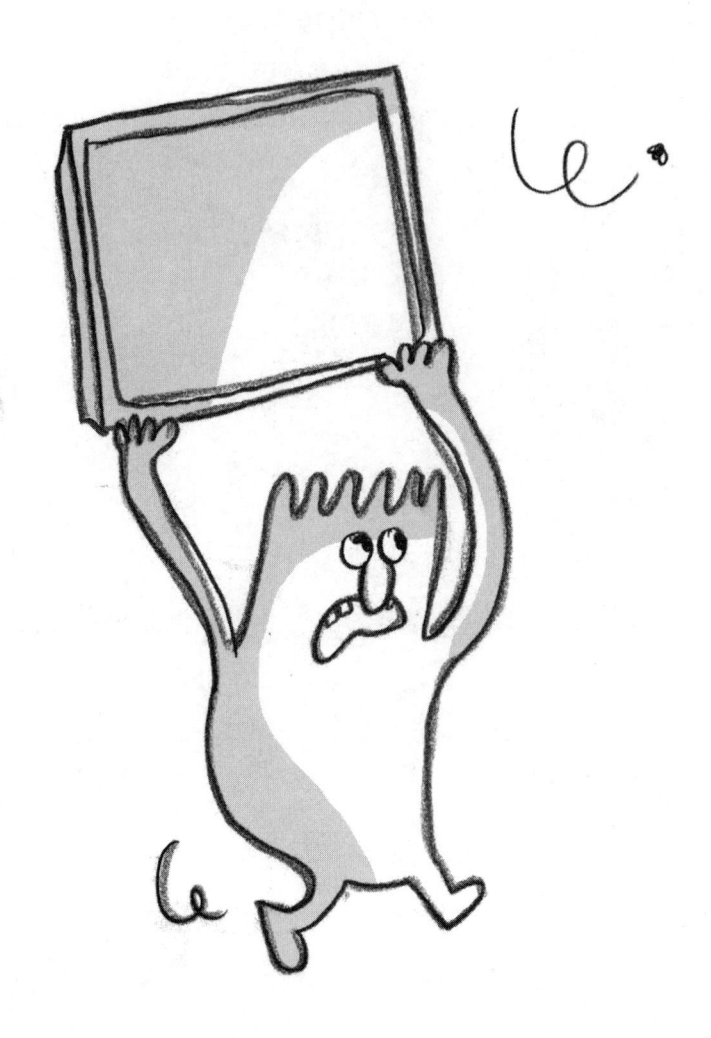

Ever tried to swat a fly with a TV?

**Why was the doctor
angry with the nurse?**

**Because he lost
his patients.**

Why don't oranges win marathons?

They run out of juice.

How do bees get to school?

SCHOOL BUZZ

They take the buzz.

What creepy crawly may you find in your shoe?

A sockroach.

What did the egg say to the banana?

Nothing, eggs can't talk!

Why did the scientist's breath smell so good?

Because he'd eaten an experi-mint.

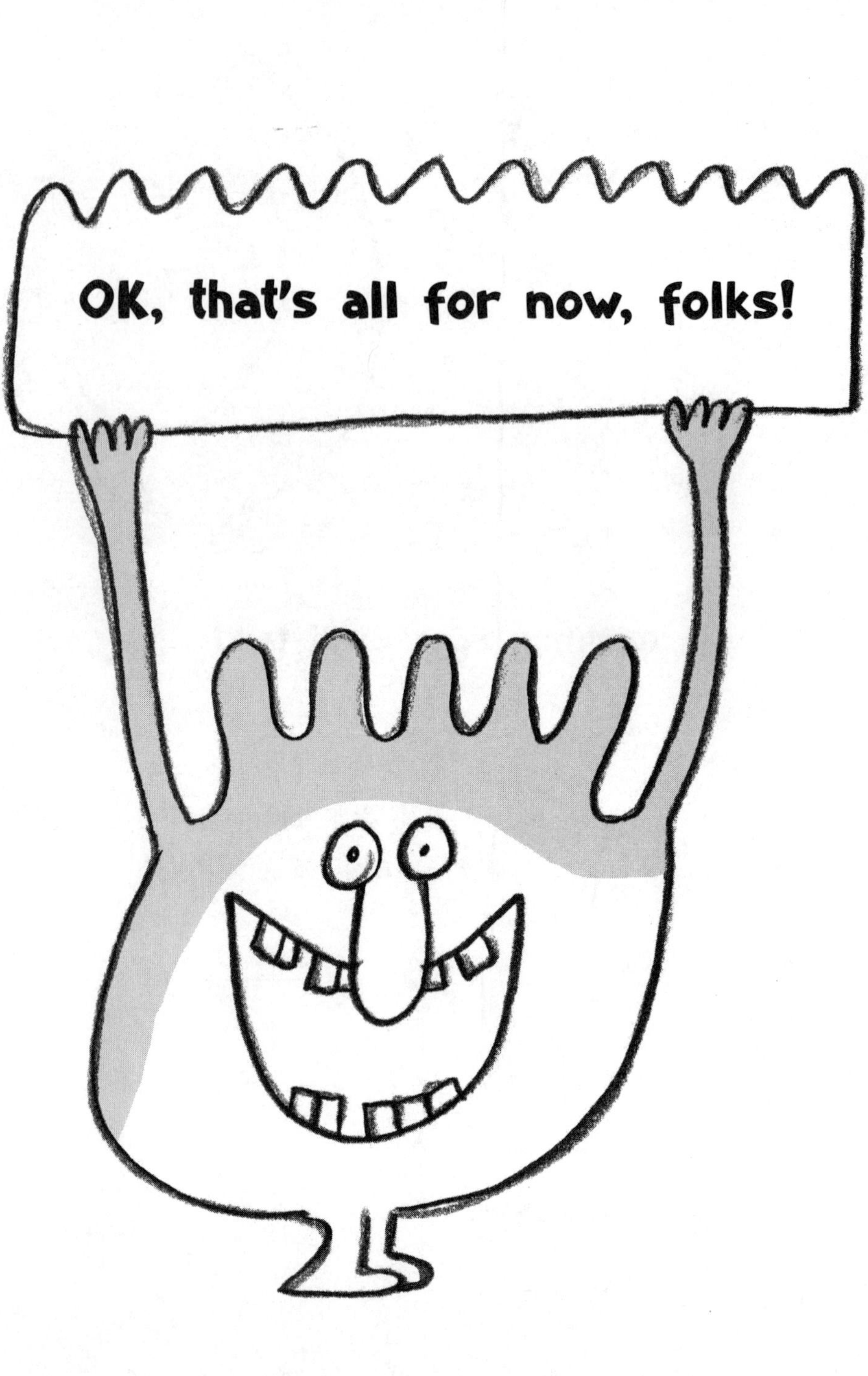
OK, that's all for now, folks!